BEYOND THE SILENCE
women's unheard voices from the Troubles

Edited by Julieann Campbell

the unHEARD VOICES

GUILDHALL PRESS

ISBN: 978 1 911053 11 8
Copyright © Creggan Enterprises, 2016.

Cover concept/design © David Campbell.
Cover image collage © Dreamstime/William Carson Collection.
Internal images © William Carson Collection, Eamon Melaugh, POAC and Hugh Gallagher.

The editor and contributors assert their moral rights in this work in accordance with the Copyright, Designs and Patents Act 1998.

First published February 2016.

Guildhall Press
Ráth Mór Business Park
Bligh's Lane, Derry
Ireland
BT48 0LZ
00 44 28 7136 4413
www.ghpress.com

Creggan Enterprises
Ráth Mór Complex
Bligh's Lane, Derry
Ireland
BT48 0LZ
00 44 28 7137 3170
www.rathmor.com

A catalogue record for this title is available from the British Library.

The conversations in the book all come from the editor's recollections, though they are not written to represent word-for-word transcripts. Rather, the editor has retold them in a way that evokes the feeling and meaning of what was said and in all instances, the essence of the dialogue is accurate. Some names and identifying details have been changed to protect the privacy of individuals.

Although the editor, publisher and Creggan Enterprises have made every effort to ensure that the information in this book was correct at press time, they do not assume and hereby disclaim any liability to any party for any loss, damage, or disruption caused by errors or omissions however made. The views and experiences expressed in this publication are not necessarily those of Creggan Enterprises or the publisher.

All rights reserved. No part of this publication may be reproduced or transmitted in any form or by any means, electronic or mechanical, including photocopy, recording, or any information storage or retrieval system, without permission in writing from the publisher. This book is distributed subject to the condition that it shall not, by way of trade or otherwise, be lent, sold or otherwise circulated without the publisher's prior consent in any form of binding or cover other than that in which it is originally published and without a similar condition to this condition being imposed on the subsequent recipient.

INTERNATIONAL FUND FOR IRELAND

RÁTH MÓR
Creggan Enterprises

the unHEARD VOICES

Acknowledgements

Creggan Enterprises would like to acknowledge and express gratitude to all those who ensured that this book has been published.

We are extremely grateful to the International Fund for Ireland and the Community Foundation for Northern Ireland, in particular Monina O'Prey, Sean Feenan and Claire O'Kane. Appreciations are also extended to the Unheard Voices steering committee members including Hilary Sidwell, Wendy McClay, Louise McIntyre, Niree McMorris, Denise Grant, Ruby McNaught and Conal McFeely. Also to Julieann Campbell who transcribed and edited the narratives, and David Campbell for designing the book cover.

A thank you, also, to CALMS who offered trauma support and to Paul and Kevin Hippsley, Joe McAllister, Garbhan Downey, Declan Carlin and Peter McCartney of Guildhall Press for offering their advice and expertise.

Finally, and most importantly, a huge thank you to all the women who welcomed us into their homes and courageously agreed to tell their stories for us to publish. We hope your voices will now be heard and listened to.

Programme Partners

The Editor
Julieann Campbell is an award-winning author and poet from Derry/Londonderry. A former reporter for the *Derry Journal* and former Chair of the Bloody Sunday Trust, her first non-fiction book, *Setting the Truth Free: The Inside Story of the Bloody Sunday Justice Campaign* (Liberties Press, 2012), won the 2013 Christopher Ewart-Biggs Memorial Prize. Other publishing credits include a poetry collection, *Milk Teeth* (Guildhall Press, 2015), and chapters in *City of Music: Derry's Music Heritage* (Guildhall Press, 2008). A keen facilitator of oral history, *Beyond the Silence* is her second non-fiction book.

Creggan Enterprises
This publication arose from the work of Creggan Enterprises, a social economy initiative committed to the overall well-being of local people and the community it seeks to promote and service. For the past twenty-five years Creggan Enterprises has been to the fore in championing inclusion and peacebuilding through the process of social and economic revival.

International Fund for Ireland
The Unheard Voices Programme is supported by the International Fund for Ireland (IFI) through its Peace Impact Programme. The IFI is an independent international organisation established by the British and Irish Governments in 1986. Financed by contributions from the United States of America, the European Union, Canada, Australia and New Zealand, the Fund promotes economic and social advance, and encourages contact, dialogue and reconciliation between nationalists and unionists throughout Ireland. At its core, the Fund's mission is to tackle the underlying causes of sectarianism and violence and to build reconciliation between people and within and between communities throughout the island of Ireland.

The IFI recognises the importance of all voices and perspectives in peacebuilding but does not endorse any specific viewpoint. The views and experiences expressed and contained in this publication are not necessarily those of the IFI.

*There is no greater agony than bearing
an untold story inside you.*

Maya Angelou

1928–2014

American author, poet, and civil rights activist.

Contents

Introduction	8
Women's Role in Peacebuilding	10
Foreword	11

Compassion in chaos
Ruby McNaught – *The saintly widow*	14
Lorraine Murray – *The red stiletto*	17
Anonymous – *I resented my mother's peace work*	21

Security forces
Anonymous – *I was an RUC man's wife, nobody spoke to me*	28
Anonymous – *A smile costs nothing*	32
Anonymous – *I felt I had to keep my job a secret*	37
Anonymous – *Every time I go over that bridge, I'm back home*	44

Absent role models
Anonymous – *He was supposed to be my daddy*	50
Colette O'Connor – *The man with the blackthorn stick*	54
Christine Robson – *The hearth was filled with my daddy's blood*	61

Lost siblings
Sharon Austin – *We didn't exist after my brother died*	70
Ursula Duddy – *My big brother was a pencil sketch that hung in our living room*	76
Eileen Fox – *We needed tickets for our own brother's funeral*	84
Kathleen Brotherton – *You could feel that a war was starting*	90
Philomena McLaughlin – *Sometimes I'm standing ironing and I just cry*	94
Tricia Duddy – *I had to share my brother with strangers*	101

Women's reflections
Ruby McNaught – *Those were the days, my friend*	108
Nan Duncan – *I picked my children's friends*	111

Hilda Campbell – *Mayhem, memory and the Bay City Rollers* — *114*
Jane McMorris – *It's good that women are beginning to talk now* — *117*
Anna Gallagher – *We felt like hostages every day* — *121*
Anonymous – *Everything seemed to change overnight* — *124*
Donna Porter – *Nobody had it easy, but that's just the way it was* — *128*
Anonymous – *Nothing has changed – people still live in fear* — *131*
Anonymous – *Burnt out of our home – by our friends* — *134*
Siobhan Gallagher – *Nobody is listening to our concerns* — *137*
Amie Gallagher – *Finding a voice in 21st-century Ireland* — *140*

Widows of war
Anonymous – *We don't talk about the past at all* — *146*
Marie Newton – *We were only beginning our lives* — *149*

Glossary — *154*

Introduction

There have been many attempts to record stories of the Troubles. But because this project focuses solely on the unheard voices of women – those who felt ready to share their intensely personal stories with the wider world – the resulting anthology is one of honest, raw emotion.

The experiences here cover many perspectives: mothers who held families together and reared families in the absence of their men; women whose husbands, fathers, brothers and sisters died tragically; women who are, or who were, wives or partners of security-force personnel and combatants, both republican and loyalist; and women who were victims of past political failures, paramilitary violence and state violence, and who still bear both mental and physical scars today.

The Unheard Voices Programme has, since its inception by Creggan Enterprises in September 2013, been working with almost 1,500 women, most of whom have been directly or indirectly affected by the Troubles in Northern Ireland. Our aim is to give a voice to those whose voices were silenced.

Creggan Enterprises, who developed this project with the support of funding from the International Fund for Ireland's Peace Impact Programme, firmly believe that women – with their central role within the home and community – are essential to peacebuilding.

Unheard Voices sought to support women who find themselves marginalised in today's post-conflict society, and to foster understanding between communities through dialogue, understanding and reconciliation.

This collection of women's testimonies is the fruit of two years' work and captures just a few of the untold stories that shape the narratives of our communities today.

This book evolved from one key strand of the Unheard Voices work – our Oral History programme – which provided a space for participants to share experiences and examine the recent history of which many of them were a part.

It has been both a very humbling and rewarding two years. As strangers in many instances, we were welcomed into homes and invited to listen as women spoke candidly of their personal experiences. Indeed, some of the following stories have been buried so deeply, they have yet to be shared with other family members.

While most of the participants used their real names, some preferred to remain anonymous to protect themselves and their families from further hurt and pain. In the majority of instances, the women were grateful that someone actually *asked* to hear their story. Many benefitted from speaking to us and found sharing cathartic, a turning point for them to start dealing with lingering hurt and pain, therefore allowing them to move on with their lives.

Many of the women we interviewed are resilient. However, others remain fragile and we found it necessary to refer many participants to seek support to cope with and manage the trauma and stress that are still very raw and evident today.

The focus of the book was quite straightforward and the invaluable assistance of trusted key women who play important roles (mostly voluntarily) within their communities enabled us to identify women who were willing to speak about their experiences. Without the help of these key figures, many interviews could not have taken place.

The majority of interviews were held in the home setting; others took place wherever the women felt most comfortable. Each testimony depended on the full approval of the individual participant, which was obviously vital to the storytelling process and ensured that women retained ownership of the process.

The stories are set out under the following themes: 'Compassion in chaos', 'Security forces', 'Absent role models', 'Lost siblings', 'Women's reflections', and 'Widows of war'.

Julieann Campbell, who compiled and edited the stories, and I feel honoured that the women entrusted us with their stories and we hope we have done them justice.

Sometimes it takes more than one voice to convey a story. It is worth remembering that for every woman's story committed to paper here, there are hundreds, perhaps thousands, more within every community that remain untold. Now is the time to hear those voices. Only through taking the time to ask, listen and understand can we begin to learn lessons from the recent past and really build a meaningful, equal and inclusive future.

Carol Cunningham
Co-ordinator of Unheard Voices

Women's Role in Peacebuilding

There is growing awareness at a global level that women have a much more significant role in peacebuilding and that strategies need to be developed to facilitate this process. Without the dynamic involvement of women at all levels in society, real progress will never be achieved.

Let's not forget that women were often the very people that held communities and families together throughout the very worst of the Troubles. While so often demonstrating strength, these women should now be supported in healing the pain suffered through years of silence. If we are to reinforce progress towards a peaceful and stable society, we simply cannot afford to lose women's voices on the urgent challenges that still exist.

Unheard Voices, supported by the International Fund for Ireland, is a powerful project that has engaged women in a unique and empowering way without shying away from difficult issues. The testimonies in this book are compelling, raw and often challenging. These are brave stories of incredible quality and personal honesty. They deserve to be heard.

Adrian Johnston
Chairman
International Fund for Ireland

Foreword

These stories, many hidden for decades, reflect the real impact of the politics of violence on the lives of women, children and communities during the last forty years. They are evidence of the immense courage of the group of women – from very diverse community backgrounds – who took part in the Unheard Voices Project, developed by Creggan Enterprises.

These testimonies provide us with important insights into the pain, hurt and struggles faced by women during the conflict of the past four decades. They show the devastation that the violence caused and the trauma left in its wake – trauma that is ongoing today.

If we are to honour these women's stories, and the countless other untold stories, we must ensure that we don't go back to the political failures and the resultant violent conflict of the past. It is time now to build a more inclusive, peaceful and equal society for the next generation – a society that seeks to address the trauma caused by the conflict and that respects and values the voice of women as fundamental to building community cohesion.

Creggan Enterprises is proud and honoured to be able to present this publication of the unheard stories suffered by women. The Unheard Voices Project was initiated and then nourished by Creggan Enterprises to enable women to have their stories heard – women whose stories and experiences have been silenced, ignored, discouraged or marginalised.

I wish to thank the International Fund for Ireland for their financial support for this initiative and to acknowledge the work of the staff involved in the delivery of the project, namely Carol Cunningham, Barbara Wosser and Joan Murray. It is also important to record our appreciation to Conal McFeely for initiating this work on the legacy of dealing with the past and to Julieann Campbell for her noteworthy editorial skills in the production of this book.

Most especially, we owe these courageous women involved with Unheard Voices a debt of gratitude for sharing their stories with us.

Anne Molloy
Chairperson
Creggan Enterprises

Compassion in chaos

I don't think it will ever go away, but I knew I'd feel some kind of relief talking about it. While it hasn't been easy, I feel like I've managed to confront the past and will hopefully be able to move on or at least deal better with what happened.

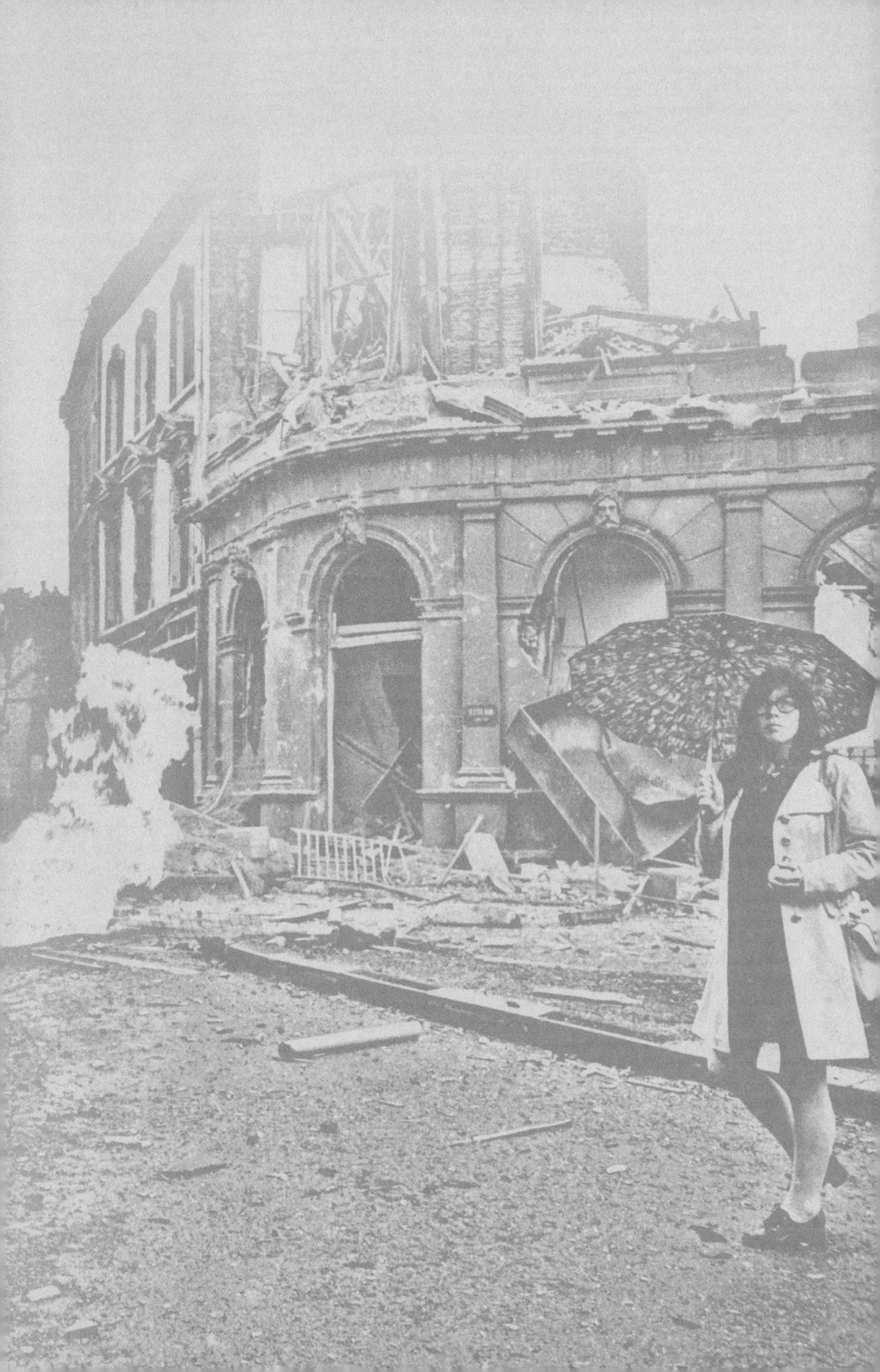

Ruby McNaught

The saintly widow

Appalling things took place during four decades of conflict, but alongside every tragedy shone tales of unimaginable bravery. This is one such story. Ruby McNaught reveals a simple act of kindness during the 1970s when her late mother, Kathleen McLaughlin, risked her own safety to bring a mortally wounded soldier into her house.

The term 'strong, independent woman' is often bandied about in the media, and, having heard it said so often, I now realise my mother was exactly this. I didn't think so when I was young, though. Back then, she was just a widow, rearing children on her own after my father died many years before. It's only now, all these years later, that I realise what a strong woman she was. She had the courage of her convictions – and where's the shame in that?

Reminiscing with my own kids about family history has helped me see just how strong Derry women were in the 1950s and 1960s. People like Bridget Bond and Mary Nelis, to name but a few. My mother was never into politics and often proclaimed to be a pacifist. She had no formal education, as was the norm in Derry then, but you couldn't do her in a shilling. She managed what little money she had in a way I never could.

My mother taught us respect for each other and the community we lived in. Through tough and troubled times, we were amazed at how she handled things. The Troubles in Derry, for many, were terrible heartbreak and tragedy. We look back now, and wonder how we ever survived them. It was our mothers – these same strong women – who led the way through those awful times.

One such incident in our lives was the death of a young British soldier, suffocated in an army Land Rover outside my mother's house on Westland Street. It was the usual Saturday night rioting, young men engaging army patrols with stones and petrol bombs. Local newspapers reported the incident at the time, inaccurately I have to say.

This young soldier died from asphyxiation while under attack from youths throwing petrol bombs on 28 February 1971 – the first British soldier to be killed in Derry. He was eighteen-year-old Lance Corporal Bill Jolliffe, on his second tour of duty in Northern Ireland. A redcap, otherwise known as the military police, who were unarmed, and had been stationed at Bligh's Lane.

The saintly widow

The patrol had finished its shift and was about to return to base when they took a detour to examine a fire in Lecky Road. This detour proved to be fatal because they were ambushed at Westland Street, at the junction between Blucher Street and Cable Street. Four petrol bombs hit the jeep and it lost control, mounting the footpath opposite my mother's house.

The driver jumped out of the jeep as it rolled over. He ran to help his comrades but, unable to do so, he left the scene. Some local people ran to the burning jeep to try to release the men trapped inside. They succeeded in opening the doors and pulling back the jeep's canvas cover to find two men unconscious and a third man hysterical in the back. It was stated later at the inquest that this third man mistook the rescuers for attackers.

He was unconscious by the time my mother and my brother-in-law Jim and others got him out of the jeep. He was lying on the ground, so my mother said, 'Please help me get him into my house, he's some mother's son. He's not going to die like a dog in the street.'

The inquest said that he died of inhaling fumes from the fire extinguisher his jeep colleagues had used to put out the fire, so his death was indirectly related to the petrol bomb attack. That night my mother cared for that young man. She knew nothing about him, except that he was some mother's son, yet still she prayed with him and tried to give him comfort as he lay there dying.

> That night my mother cared for that young man. She knew nothing about him, except that he was some mother's son, yet still she prayed with him and tried to give him comfort as he lay there dying.

This story of helping someone in distress took a cruel twist when my mother and family then suffered a vicious hate campaign, which lasted several months. She would wake every morning to find the front door painted with slogans. She bought a tin of paint and painted it over. The windows were broken regularly, but she just replaced them. She got death threats, and people shouted insults at her in the street and intimidated her. The hate campaign was vile.

The Housing Trust offered to rehouse her, but no – she had such strength of character and refused to leave the area where she had been born and bred. After four months, the hate campaign stopped as quickly as it had started. My mother had won, through her courage and determination, and she knew that what she did that night was the right thing to do for her and for that soldier's family.

My mother was nonviolent in her approach to life, despite living on one of the front lines of the Troubles. Those who knew her respected her views. Her funeral was a humbling experience by its sheer size and the high esteem in which she was held. Young men who had served time in Long Kesh approached us. They told us that my mother had sent them parcels in prison. We'd never known that.

My mother was in the peace movement and travelled all over Ireland to the peace rallies, I think she would be overjoyed at the peace process and the changes in the city today. She never did anyone a bad turn. She really was a strong woman who believed in following your instincts and doing what you think is right, no matter what.

Lorraine Murray

The red stiletto

On Hallowe'en night in 1993, Lorraine Murray and her mother were having a drink in the Rising Sun Bar in County Derry when UDA loyalist gunmen entered and opened fire on customers. The 'Greysteel Massacre' left seven dead and a further twelve people injured. Another died later. Despite them both being injured in the attack, these women felt abandoned and forgotten in the decades since. Only now, over twenty years later, does Lorraine openly speak of her ordeal in the hope of moving on. Silently haunted, Lorraine truly is one of this island's unheard voices.

When I was twenty-seven and my youngest son was three months old, I started to develop bad postnatal depression, and so my mother insisted I needed a night out to lift my head. She said she was taking me out for a drink – that's how my mother and I ended up there.

My da drove us and we got there around 9.00pm. There weren't many people there – it was a quiet little bar with no fuss for Hallowe'en – that's why we went there. I ran into the bar to check what time it was over for my da to collect us. We didn't know it at the time, but *they* were actually parked right behind my da's car at that point.

We were standing at the bar and I remember joking about where we'd find a seat because it was so empty in the bigger lounge area. Then, as we walked towards a table, the gunmen came in behind us. One of them shouted 'Trick or treat' and a young girl said to him, 'That isn't even funny,' and he just shot her where she sat. Shot her in the face or head … She was younger than me, only a teenage girl. Thank God, I didn't know anybody in there, which kind of helps a bit …

The shooting seemed to go on forever. You don't even have thoughts; you hadn't the time to think. We just dived under the table and I lay with my hands over my head. I thought if I lay as if I was dead, they would believe it. I remember thinking, 'Not my face.'

Cartridges were falling on the floor from the gunman beside me and the smell was very strong. When his gun went quiet, I looked up and he was either reloading the rifle or it had jammed because he was doing something at the side of it – that was when we started crawling on our stomachs underneath all the tables towards the fire exit.

It all happened so fast. When I looked back my mother was nowhere to be seen – she had fallen at the door and so I went back to get her. That's when I was shot, too. She kept saying, 'I can't, I can't,' but eventually I got her to her feet. My mother was shot in the stomach, too, but the bullet had bounced off her handbag first, so it wasn't too bad an injury.

We ran towards a housing estate and as we were trying to run up the path, I felt the gunmen behind us watching us. I was so scared to look back I just carried on, wearing one red stiletto shoe – in TV footage you can see my one red shoe lying inside in the middle of the floor.

> My mother was only in her fifties when it happened, but she was never right afterwards. It wrecked her nerves, wrecked her life. She never went out or did anything.

My arm felt heavy like a dead arm and there was blood dripping from it. I only knew one house so we ran to their door. They didn't believe us to start with and thought we were joking because it was Hallowe'en, until I showed them my arm and said, 'Does it look like I'm joking?'

The ambulance came to us at the house first before it found out what had happened at the bar. Then we sat outside in the ambulance while they went in to help. They were bringing people out on stretchers and there was a lot of blood, and there were TV cameras everywhere, too, and people all standing around.

My mother wasn't injured badly, thank God. It was a clean wound and they stitched her up. The bullet came off her handbag and across her – and that had probably saved her. I don't think she even realised she had been shot until the ambulance men checked her over. They couldn't close my two wounds so I had to go to casualty every day. But I still got away lightly, compared to some.

My mother, Mary 'Nila' McKeever, was only in her fifties when it happened, but she was never right afterwards. It wrecked her nerves, wrecked her life. She never went out or did anything. She always had this guilt that she took me out and this happened – she often said that – but we never really talked about it again properly afterwards. She did mention it sometimes, but I never said a word about it. I had three children and just got on with it.

News reports said afterwards that they wanted to speak to a woman seen going into the bar and leaving again before the shooting started. That was me – checking what time the place closed – so I had to come forward to the police and eliminate myself.

The red stiletto

I locked myself in the house for the guts of two years, and for the first year, I think I had my doors locked all the time, still worrying that they would come back to get us. Eventually, my father said enough was enough, and he took me to see a counsellor, but it didn't work for me. Nobody understood. They just sat there, expecting me to talk and I couldn't talk, so I never went back. I just went home and got on with it. My children were all under six, and I couldn't even hold my youngest baby for months afterwards because I wasn't supposed to use the arm.

I remember the months and years afterwards more than the night itself. I took bad panic attacks for over a year. I remember the feeling of fear – I wouldn't answer the door, close my blinds, or sit with my back to a door. Not a chance. I still won't go into rural bars.

It left a massive mental scar as well as the physical one. I'm still attending hospital yet with the arm, but physical stuff I can deal with. Even today, I won't sit with my back to a window or door, and don't close the blinds after it gets dark because I have to be able to see who comes near my door. When I go in anywhere, I still always look around to see where the exits are. I still never celebrate Hallowe'en, and I have a fear of the dark, too.

Because my mother and I didn't live in Greysteel, we were forgotten about. I was managing all right until the 20th anniversary when it was all over the TV and in the newspapers. Then there was trouble locally and gun threats and it all just triggered it again. I'd never had antidepressants in my life, but I went on them then, that's how bad I felt.

I've always been too overprotective of my children since. They say I have a condition – a fear of everything. They didn't know about what happened for a long time, I didn't want them to know. It took a long time to let them play outside properly.

When they grew up and started heading into the town at night, I was a torture. I would text, ring, and sit up late waiting and worrying. Thankfully, they always let me know where they were, and that they had left the town. I could relax as long as I knew they were out of the town. I hated them going out at night.

Last year was my first time out on Hallowe'en since it happened. I used to sit with my mother every year until she died, because she hated Hallowe'en so much, too, but this year I went to my daughter's house and watched the fireworks with her. She texted my partner to say, 'I'm so proud of her!' I didn't even stay there very long, but at least I went …

It's strange, but the children in my street don't come near my door on Hallowe'en night, either. Maybe their parents have told them about me and they just stay away, but I buy sweets in every year, just in case.

It felt raw around the anniversary. I saw the commemoration on TV and was glad I didn't go. If my mother was alive maybe I would have went, but she died nine years ago. I feel worse about it all now that my ma's not here, it was all right when there was two of us, but now that it's just me …

It took years before I could set foot in a bar again. I did go back into the bar in Greysteel once, years later, when my partner persuaded me to go to a darts tournament there; he said I had to face it. The journey back there that night was horrible, and the minute I stepped inside, I could still see everything as it was that night: the people, the blood, everything. I could still see the people lying there. I drank and drank that night, but just couldn't get drunk.

The time is right to talk about it now. It feels like my mother and I weren't even there. When they talk about Greysteel – we're not included. It's as if we were never there. They offered nothing but a counsellor when it happened and then they forgot about us.

There *were* outsiders there, but nobody ever mentions that or contacts us about anything, like we didn't matter. You talk about unheard voices. That's me and my mother … nobody ever asked or cared afterwards. I wouldn't even have known about the memorial if I hadn't seen it on the news on TV.

Looking back now, it feels as though it all happened to someone else. To this day, not a lot of people know. Close family and some neighbours maybe. I hope I will get over it eventually. It feels like I should be talking about it now, however hard it might be. Maybe that's what was wrong – I never did talk to anyone about it. My daddy said to me once, 'You need a good cry – you've never cried,' and he was right. I'm sure he must have felt quite helpless at times.

I don't think it will ever go away, but I knew I'd feel some kind of relief talking about it. The only reason I have talked about it now is because of the Unheard Voices Project. While it hasn't been easy, I feel like I've managed to confront the past and will hopefully be able to move on or at least deal better with what happened.

Anonymous

I resented my mother's peace work

History hails the brave individuals who paved the path to peace in Northern Ireland, but few realise the fear faced by their families at home. Behind the headlines, activists' families were often harassed and intimidated by sinister forces, their children tormented. Londonderry woman 'Laura' (not her real name) lived with fear from an early age, which, she now acknowledges, led to resentment of her mother's role in the early peace movement. For the first time, Laura reflects on the emotional price of peace.

I'm the second youngest of five children. We lived all over the Waterside and in the Fountain, too, but my most impressionable period was when we moved to a bigger loyalist estate when I was six. Those years had the greatest impact on my life.

My father was in the Territorial Army, and my mother was one of the people who started a group called the Peace Movement in the mid-1970s. I was about eight when the movement started up and it was a cross-community project, Catholics and Protestants working together.

My mother wanted a different life for us – all we had ever known were bombs and trouble – but in fact, my mother's peace work was one of the worst times in my life. She was trying to do her best, and even met the Queen once, but she never realised the effect it had on us.

What stands out most is a memory of being in hysterics as a young girl. We used to get mysterious phone calls to the house from a payphone, and if I answered, a voice would say, 'Your mother is lying down the road, riddled with bullets in her head,' or, 'Your mother's murdered and lying in a field.'

It wasn't just one or two phone calls; this was throughout her whole campaign. I was only young, and I just went hysterical. We used to run squealing to my granny's house down the street, and she would bring us back up home.

I remember my mother came home a few times with her wedding ring all twisted into her finger where someone was rough with her. Other times, she would have black eyes where men or women had hit her – all because she was out there trying to bring about peace through this movement.

I was always very proud of her, but I don't remember her being there for us much. I asked her about it once, and she said, 'I have a lot to answer for,

Laura. I did a lot of things for other people while my own children were suffering.' She didn't realise all this at the time – she thought she was trying to make things better.

Besides the threatening phone calls, our windows were smashed all the time, too. We lived in the front row, opposite a Catholic area, but I don't think the hassle was because we were Protestant – it was because of my mother's work – because she was trying to change things in the 1970s when people weren't ready for change.

I don't know who was behind the phone calls, but I can still hear them to this day. I think I answered about four or five of these calls as a young girl, but the first one will be stuck in my memory forever: 'She's down the road, riddled with bullets in her head.'

That was a very bad time. I remember for a few years I ran around with my hood up and a big duffle coat on, even in the summer. It was as though I was trying to hide away and disguise myself so people wouldn't see me – in case they knew who my mother was.

I have three sisters and one brother, but I don't know if they had the same issues as me, hiding away all the time. I was so involved in my own emotions, I didn't notice. The trouble was just part of our everyday lives. I remember the bombs, and how on the bus into town, soldiers would board the bus and make people stand up to check their bags or search them. I was only nine or ten, but that happened all the time. It was just standard procedure.

I remember the checkpoints, too, particularly Shipquay Street, because they had turnstiles at the bottom of the street and tables where they would check your bags on the way through. That was just the way we lived.

Other things happened that affected us, too. A shopkeeper we knew was murdered when I was about seventeen. He was a Reserve policeman and I had spoken to him half an hour before republicans came in and shot him. I remember he'd asked me if I wanted some old magazines, which I did. He was such a lovely man. Another strong recollection I have is of someone planting a bomb under a car near where we lived, and the bomb fell off onto the street. It exploded just as a neighbour was walking home from the shop and he was blown up. That really affected us.

༓ ☽ ༓

I have nothing against anyone, which I think is my mother's influence. She would never have tolerated any disrespect towards Catholics or anyone else.

I resented my mother's peace work

Although, I was scared to go to the shops as a girl because you would be called a 'Jaffa bastard' in the street, or get thumped on the way past by both girls and fellas. I love going to the Twelfth celebrations, and my Catholic best friend comes with me every year and we end up in the Services Club afterwards. They might not know who she is – and I wouldn't go broadcasting it, either – but we still go everywhere together. We respect each other's traditions. My children also have that same sense of respect and equality.

I'm so glad my children didn't grow up in the same environment I did. They've never even heard a bomb and I think if they did hear one, they would probably die themselves. To us, it was everyday life to hear a boom and say, 'I wonder where that was?' It's hard to believe that children as young as we were would recognise the sound of bombings, but we did. We knew exactly what they were.

> I'm so proud of my mum – she was such a great woman, but I did resent her when I was younger. I wondered why she was bothering about this peace movement and not about us.

My three children were born in 1987, 1993 and 2000, and they don't know much about the Troubles. I do tell them the odd thing, but I'm not sure I'd want them to know too much. I never want them to be bitter. My son had no problem settling down with a Catholic girl, and now they have a child and are happy, so hopefully I've brought them up right. I can only do my best.

I have a fear of people in my company talking about religion. I dread to see it coming into conversation, especially when there's drink involved. I hate it. I still try to stay out of the town, too, because I hate people asking where you are from. It always tends to happen in bars. It's okay at the start of the night when people know where you're from, but at the end of the night that changes.

My husband and I have started going over the border to little hotels in Donegal for a drink instead. We stay overnight and the people there are lovely. Nobody asks where you're from, and nobody cares if you say Derry or Londonderry – you can just enjoy yourself.

I'm so proud of my mum – she was such a great woman, but I did resent her when I was younger. I wondered why she was bothering about this peace movement and not about us. With my da, it was happy times, being up on his back and lots of fun; but with my mother it was all meetings and drama. I resented that, and I used to play up a lot. I wished she wouldn't go to meetings, and I dreaded those phone calls …

It took many years before I could talk to my mother about it all, and when I finally did, the nicest thing she ever said was sorry. She hadn't realised how things were for us back then. Until then, she had never acknowledged any of it, and I knew I couldn't go any further until she did. In the end, we grew very close and I used to visit her three times a day.

I'm glad that I have talked about this today, while I can, because it will disappear again. I will suppress it, though it's always there. I don't think I have ever talked about this as openly as I have today, and it's been very emotional. It feels like a lot off my mind.

I'm a stronger person for my mother being in that peace movement. It could have turned out so much worse, but today I am happy, and I know she did her best. My mother said in a magazine article at the time, 'We've got to make something better for the children, they're the most important.' She always had strong principles like that, and she always worked in the community.

I suppose I didn't realise back then what she was trying to do. The 1970s were a bad time, and that peace movement were some of the first to come out on the streets and try – for the city.

Security forces

I never thought I would speak about these experiences, but maybe the time is right. I know too many people who now see psychiatrists because of the things they've seen in the past. It's hard to think that this is such a tiny island, yet there are people doing that to each other.

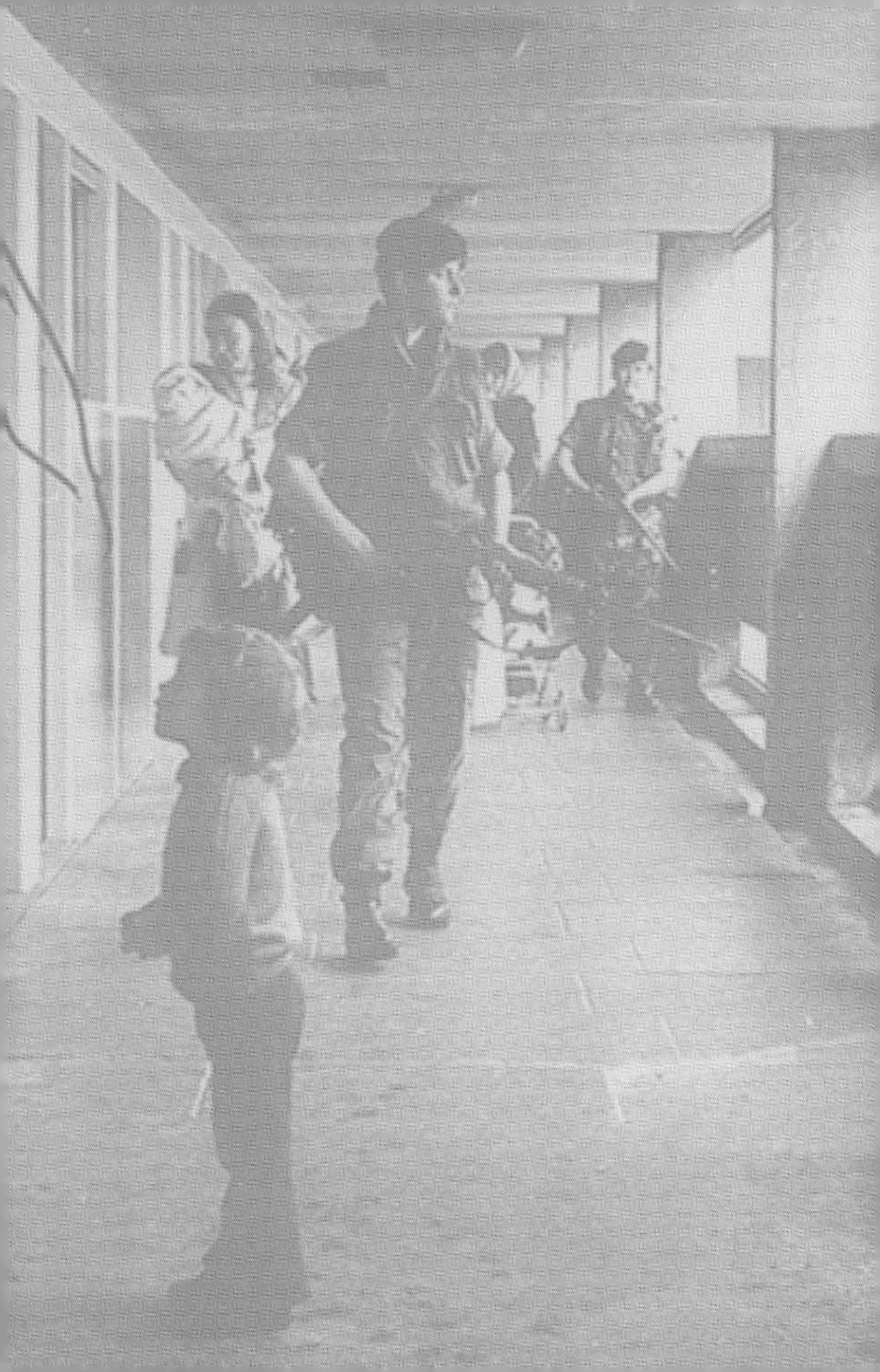

Anonymous

I was an RUC man's wife, nobody spoke to me

Few can imagine the isolation and fear felt by the wives and families of RUC officers serving in the North throughout the civil unrest. For one local woman, who wishes to remain anonymous, the pressure of being an RUC wife permeated every aspect of her life and personality. She reflects on this experience and on the liberation felt since her marriage ended. All names have been changed.

I met my ex-husband 'Ken' in my teens, and he was the only man I loved. We went steady and fell in and out, but we kept coming back together. He worked locally but applied to join the RUC and was accepted.

He left for the training depot the week after our engagement, and from then on, I only saw him at weekends. I knew I would worry, but I had great faith and always believed that the hand of God would be upon him. It was something he wanted to do – he wanted to serve the community and he thought it was right to do it. I was the typical woman, I accepted whatever he wanted to do, and we got married.

In the RUC, you need police permission to marry and they did all sorts of background checks on my family and me before they'd allow the marriage. We were granted permission because we were getting married in the countryside, which was considered safe enough.

Afterwards, we went to Scotland for our honeymoon, there was no such thing as foreign holidays in those days. We had no car, no money, and we didn't go far. This was in the early 1970s, and I remember Ken used to bus it home on a Friday night. He got home at 10.00pm and was away again on Sunday.

When we came home from honeymoon, we heard we'd been allocated a house in a place I'd never heard of. We packed up the few things we had and left. We had no money, and when we got there, I went to a supermarket for some food and it was the first time I had ever counted pennies. Until then, my mother had provided everything for me, and I remember that moment in time so well – the realisation that we really were on our own. I found that hard.

Ken was stationed in a border town and we were told that no police wives would be allowed to live there because it was such a high security risk, so we lived outside the town where it was safe. We never saw our men. They were working eighteen hours a day and you just had to get on with it. I was very homesick the first year because he was always working, and that was dreadful. People in the town never spoke to you or said hello, the way people do in the city, but my mammy and daddy came to visit me sometimes.

There were difficult times, and you never knew who was who – so nobody mixed. In that way, it was never a community as such. Everyone was very wary and kept to themselves. Because I was living in a border town, and I was an RUC man's wife, nobody spoke to me. Even Protestants – your own community – didn't want to know you because you were police.

People tend to think it was only Catholics who hated the police, but Protestant people didn't want to know you, either. Nobody wanted to be your friend. They were frightened, because if they were to associate with you they could be targeted, too. Sometimes people didn't even want to travel with you in the car, such was the fear at that time.

> Police families and wives didn't exactly communicate with each other. They didn't make friends or visit each other's houses. You met them in the street and said hello; that was about it.

My husband was then transferred to a town in the east, which was classed as a republican town, so the RUC wives and families had to live in nearby towns or villages. Police families and wives still didn't exactly communicate with each other. They didn't make friends or visit each other's houses. You met them in the street and said hello; that was about it.

One woman told me that I would make friends at the school gates once I had children, and she was right, but it was very isolating being the wife of a policeman. I was very young and very alone. I had a miscarriage, too, which was really difficult.

We always had to be careful. You didn't say what time your husband was on duty, or what time he would be home. You just didn't talk about those things. You never knew when he would be home – it could be hours or days. I did worry, there was always that fear, but I hoped that the hand of God would be upon him, and it was, thankfully. It kept him safe.

When we moved towns again, we made friends with some of the wives there who were a bit friendlier. An awful lot of Protestants had left cities because of the Troubles and it did feel safer. We lived there for years in a police house, and when our first child was born, Ken was working his usual eighteen hours a day.

I remember when I went into labour they wouldn't let me give birth in the hospital until the GP came on at 8.00am the next morning. There was an army wife from Ballykelly in hospital with me, too, and I really felt for her because the army wives in Ballykelly really *were* isolated. They were usually English or Scottish girls – over here all on their own – and so I used to sit and talk to her a lot.

Northern Ireland was split into police divisions, so we had to go where Ken was sent. We had always wanted to come back to Londonderry, but, of course, in the RUC you couldn't live in your own town or even in the same county. So we moved again and I gave birth three weeks after moving.

I cocooned my children and they were with me twenty-four hours a day. I always kept them safe and sheltered from things. They didn't get out in the street, either, which had its drawbacks because they weren't very streetwise.

Nothing changed in the new house, though. Nobody wanted to know you because you were a policeman's wife and they were a policeman's children. We had to get used to checking under the car for bombs every morning – that went on for years. Our doors were always locked, too, and you never left the key in the door. We lived like that all our lives. Naturally, we didn't tell the children these things. It was just the way things were.

We stayed there for four years. Once, we came back from holidays to find two well-dressed detectives waiting on the doorstep to inform us that terrorists had put a threat on our house. A list had been found, and our address and house number was on it. So we had to move. My father wanted them to transfer us closer to home, but Ken decided that we should stay where we were, so we got bulletproof windows and an intercom put in. Back then, terrorists were actually going into homes and holding wives hostage, but we had faith and we were okay. My husband later left the RUC and we came back home to Londonderry and settled with no regrets.

When the marriage broke up, I had no friends. My kids were my life. I had lived that way for so long, it was all I knew, and so when my marriage ended, my personality changed, too. I find I have become more open, more accepting, and freer. I'm more open-minded nowadays. I'm very straight with people, and I expect everybody else to be truthful, too. I think it's important to always be honest with people and I strive to do so.

I never would have chosen to end my marriage. Being a policeman's wife was really hard and difficult, but life has been good to me, considering. Once

I began getting out and joining women's groups, my whole life improved. I have met so many wonderful people – friends of all backgrounds – and I doubt I would have done that if I were still married. That probably sounds daft, but it's true. I wouldn't have joined a group or mixed with people very much at all. Now I feel I can air my views without fear, I have nothing to prove to anyone.

I really like the fact that the city is being called Derry/Londonderry nowadays. I like the name Londonderry, and I do say Derry, too. I'm quite comfortable with that. But if you ask me where I'm from, I'd say Londonderry. There is a healthy interest in each other's cultures beginning now, too, which is great to see.

I think it's lovely that a person like me – someone from the Waterside – can rush over to the Creggan to be here like I did today for this interview. Things have progressed so much, and I think that's an awful lot to do with the women in this city, the community groups and all the work that goes on behind the scenes. I hope they go home at night and instil that same strength in their children, too.

We're not isolated like we used to be. We're all working together now, and we work well together.

Anonymous

A smile costs nothing

Born in a village near County Tyrone, 'Catherine' (not her real name) had no idea she would spend a lifetime caring for others, or as an army wife whose husband fought in the Gulf War. Having spent twenty-two years away from Ireland, Catherine now reflects on her experiences as a wife, mother and carer, and her decision to return to her family homestead.

I had always wanted to do nursing, but worked in a factory as a girl. Although I was a Protestant, religion didn't matter much to me then. My two friends were from Gobnascale and Creggan and it just didn't matter. We used to go to the Casbah Bar to see the Undertones, and I would have gone to the Bogside Inn with them, too. It was all good banter. People might say, 'She's a Prod, get her out!' But it was more for a laugh occasionally, nothing serious.

I left the factory and went to work in the sterilising department of Altnagelvin Hospital until I got into Pupil Nurse Training. Halfway through my training, I became pregnant and, as I was only nineteen, I had the baby adopted. It just wouldn't have worked. My mum died when I was six, and I had two brothers, so I would have had to depend on people looking after us, so I knew I either had to have the baby adopted or give up my nursing. It was the right thing to do at that time. I have never regretted the decision, although I'd really love to see her someday. She would be thirty-four now.

After I finished my nursing course, there were no jobs available, so the factory offered me work in the meantime, which was brilliant. That saw me working back in the factory for another two years. I was briefly engaged to a man around then, too, but he was bad news, and six weeks after finishing with him, I was living in Jersey – so that was that.

I don't know what it was that first took me to Jersey. I had heard people talking about it and I just had this feeling about it, so I went there on my own. I didn't know anybody, and I absolutely loved it! I met other people living out there, and I met my husband, Roger, there. He was stationed near Southampton when I met him and had been visiting Jersey with the military band to play a function.

We got engaged after a year, and then married, but there was always that underlying issue of him being a Scottish Catholic and me being Protestant, as well as him being in the British Armed Forces. When we got married in 1988, many places were out of bounds for my husband and his regimental mates when they came for the wedding. That must have been quite scary for them really.

Although Roger was from Scotland, his Polish mother was obviously very proud of their Catholic heritage. Whenever we visited Scotland with the children in later years, she used to love us all going to Mass on a Sunday. I suppose we are pretty mixed – I am Irish, my husband is Scottish, we have a Polish name and of our two sons, one boy was born in Germany, the other was born in England!

I spent four years in Jersey and after that we went to Germany to live at an army base between Hamburg and Hannover, where we stayed for five years and I got a job for the army as a civilian nurse in the British Military Hospital there.

I remember one day being on the ward, probably around 1990, and hearing a massive explosion at a barracks in Hannover. Someone said it was thunder, but I knew it wasn't and said, 'That was not thunder – that's a bomb,' and I was right. There were a couple of car-bomb explosions over there as well, because the IRA were bombing the British forces in Germany, too. Hearing bombs in the distance again just brought me right back to hearing them here.

Because of this terrorist threat, there was heightened security. We had to check our car every morning and they gave us special mirrors to check underneath for bombs. No matter what you were doing, even if you had your children in your arms, you still always had to stop and check before even thinking about getting into your car. That went on for months.

We were warned to look out for devices that looked like black VHS video cassettes, as that's what some bombs looked like. You had to get to know your car so you could spot anything unusual. You couldn't even touch it until you had searched it first, even just going to the shops and back. Even though I was brought up with all that here, it is strange to think it still affected me over in Germany.

I left the British Military Hospital to work at the Medical Centre there. By then, the first Gulf War had just begun and the Iraqis had invaded Kuwait and my husband Roger was sent out there for six months with his brigade.

We said our goodbyes the morning he left for the Gulf War, and I discovered I was pregnant shortly after he left and had to let him know in the desert. It was terrible, because you didn't know if they'd come back in one piece. His parents were in Scotland, and I was in Germany on my own really.

When I let him know about the baby, because he had married a Protestant, he wanted to find a priest in the desert. The army didn't know if they were going to live or die out in that desert, and so provided all the different denominations with their own army chaplain. So Roger somehow found a Mass in the desert and went along and spoke to the priest afterwards, explaining about marrying a Protestant and the priest gave him absolution. Ha-ha, he probably said something like, 'I forgive you for marrying an Orange woman!'

It was tough being in Germany while he was out fighting the Gulf War, but I still had my job and I just had to get on with things. Then, one day I was invited for lunch with Princess Diana! Two people from each regiment were picked to go and meet her on a visit and I was lucky enough to be chosen. We went there, and we were told whom she would speak to among us, but when she was going around, she came straight over, sat down beside me, and chatted away. She asked what I was doing for Christmas and if I was going home. I explained that I was a nurse and had to cover the Medical Centre, and she said, 'Well, I suppose someone has to do it. I hope you get home in the New Year.' Lady Diana was just beautiful. She had such lovely, sparkling eyes and was stunning up close. The morning she died I nearly broke my heart.

> We had to check our car every morning and they gave us special mirrors to check underneath for bombs ... We were warned to look out for devices that looked like black VHS video cassettes, as that's what some bombs looked like.

While I was in Germany, I had to deliver a baby once, too. It was an emergency and one of the wives delivered all of a sudden, standing up, and I had to catch the baby on my knee! I hadn't even done any midwifery, but still, it had to be done. It was wonderful, the most natural thing in the world. They named the child after me because I delivered her ...

As part of the deal, every army wife got a free flight home, and at the airfield they made an announcement that ladies should use the toilet before boarding the flight. Thank God I did, too – because I was pregnant, and it turned out I was flown home on one of those giant Hercules military transport planes.

I was the only woman on the plane, there were no seats and our suitcases were thrown into a big net. There was a toilet on board, but I'm not sure if it was a bucket or what, as a curtain around it covered it. I think we just sat on the floor all the way home, and I remember thinking to myself, 'Only I would end up going home in a bloody Hercules!' That was some experience. I laugh about it still. At least I could tell my son he was in a Hercules inside my tummy.

Eventually Roger came back from the Gulf War and the regiment were posted to Yorkshire. The boys were going on exercise again, and, again, we said our goodbyes that morning, and nine months later, we had a second child. The army has a lot to answer for, sending their men away!

In North Yorkshire, I took bad postnatal depression after my second son. I was on my own a lot, and I had two wee boys with only thirteen months between them. One day I just started crying, and all I wanted was my mum, which was impossible because my mum was dead. When people say about a pool of tears, this really was a pool – I just could not stop crying. This breakdown ended in me being in a psychiatric hospital for six weeks. My youngest was only six weeks old, so he came in with me.

I was gradually let out on weekend release and the doctors gave me great support, getting me help and childminders. The army were very good to us, too, they gave Roger all the time off we needed.

I came home sometime around that New Year, and while I was home, I could feel myself slipping backwards, back into the depression. It turned out that I actually had an underactive thyroid, and that had been the cause of many of the problems. Maybe if I knew earlier, things would have been different. I might still have had the postnatal depression, but it might not have been so severe.

Roger was with me during all those tough times, they didn't send him away because he was needed at home with me. Then, the military bands were being reorganised and Roger opted for voluntary redundancy and got out of the army after almost eighteen years. The army was his life. It was his family, and the transition afterwards was very hard on him. He missed the guys and that support network that he was used to. He missed the music, too, and tried to keep that up through the Territorial Army Band, but once we had the children, I think his priorities changed and he didn't want to go away anymore. It broke his heart to leave us.

He tried different businesses after that. I was still a SEN then – a State Enrolled Nurse – and so I went to Queen's and did my conversion to become a RGN – a Registered General Nurse. I went up a grade, but the hours were still long and in shifts, but that's nursing. I've been nursing now for thirty-four years. I started in 1979, working in orthopaedics, and I saw a lot of bone-related injuries and men coming in with bullet wounds, especially a lot of young men. I don't know how one human being can do that to another.

I always had this hankering to go back home, and after ten years living near Belfast, Roger finally agreed. We moved home around 2004 and he applied for the ambulance service. Thankfully, he never came across any animosity here, and has never had any fear about going anywhere really. I was never brought up to be bitter. I liked my Protestant heritage but none of that matters in reality. Working in the hospital, you couldn't be biased.

It felt good to be home after all those years, but it was strange, too. People would talk to me in the street, but I wouldn't remember their names. You never forget your roots, though, and we're settled now. No more travelling around. Roger and I both worked hard, but we've made it. We encouraged each other when we needed it, and we both have good jobs now. I have no regrets. I have made so many good friends over the years, and I'm still in touch with my friends from the factory here, in Jersey, and the army wives in Germany and England.

I suppose I am a positive person. I was only six years old when my mother died, so I have had it tough, but life is what you make it. Let's face it, we come in with nothing and we go out with nothing – so let's make the best of it. Who cares where you come from? Or if you are Catholic or Protestant? Respect each other regardless. There is only one God, and we will have to answer to him someday. That's what I think anyway.

As long as you live a good life, that's all that counts. I always say a smile costs nothing, and that really is important – to just smile at someone and have them smile back at you.

Anonymous

I felt I had to keep my job a secret

From 1969 onwards, a sizeable section of the population was displaced by the intensity of the conflict here – all communities have been affected. 'Elizabeth', who prefers to remain anonymous, was one of many who reluctantly made the move in Derry/Londonderry. She then spent seventeen years as an RUC reservist, witnessing the horror of the Troubles first-hand.

I'm a Protestant born and bred on the west bank in the Rosemount area of the city. My parents had a business there for many years before they moved out of the area in the mid-1970s because of the Troubles. Rosemount was peaceful for my sisters and me in those early years. It was a mixed area back then, but the Troubles had started and there was an influx of Roman Catholics to the district. With our proximity to the Creggan housing estate, it became apparent that, at that time, they were by no means sympathetic to us being Protestant.

Windows were broken in our house constantly; my father's car windows were smashed, as well as the plate glass windows in the shop on numerous occasions. We eventually fitted grills to the shop windows. My sister's husband, who was in the RUC, was assaulted at gunpoint whilst visiting us in 1972 and the situation made it impossible for them to visit us again. Likewise, when my eldest sister and her husband came to visit us, the army had to escort them safely out of the area, too.

We slept on the top floor of our three-storey house, and because we were so close to Creggan, we could hear the bin lids being banged, warning people when the army was coming in. I was only thirteen or so, but at night, I heard actual gunfire and returning fire and I would be lying there, petrified, thinking it sounded so close by. Looking back now, it *was* close by – just a stone's throw away really.

It felt to me like all Protestants were being intimidated at that time. However, when word spread that my parents had put the house up for sale and were moving, quite a few mothers from Creggan and the Bog came to say how disappointed they were that we were leaving. My mother had customers from all over the city, so it was good for her to know she would be missed.

We often had bomb scares in the shop, too. I can remember the army coming in and telling Mum and me to search the shop and to get out and show them if we found anything suspicious. That happened quite a few times, but we never found anything. I remember once being put out, and when we were given the all clear to go back in, we couldn't find my father anywhere. When we got back inside, there was my dad sitting by the fire with a boiled egg and toast. 'Nobody's putting me out of my house,' he said. Calm as anything.

We lived near an army base and after an IRA explosion there around October 1971 my mum and sister went up to see the damage. It was awful. Two young soldiers were killed, and my mother remembered people clapping and jeering as the army tried to remove the bodies.

When I was about sixteen I left a job in the city centre, and shortly after that, my old workplace was blown up. They were now working from portable cabins since the bombing, and I called in a few weeks later to see how they all were. When I rang the bell at the gate, a young guy answered. I remember his face to this day, he only looked about seventeen, and me thinking, 'Who are you, and what are you doing here?' and suddenly he pulled out a gun with a silencer and said, 'Get down, now.'

He took me inside where the rest of the office staff were lying on the floor. He had the gun to my head, and his hand was shaking. He was so young, and I remember thinking, 'He's going to shoot, he's going to pull that trigger.' I had visited at the worst time as they were holding up the business.

They eventually got their money. I remember that the office manager actually had the keys to the safe down her knickers. We were telling her to give him the keys. Eventually, she did hand them over, and they got what they wanted and away they went. One of my former colleagues later took me home in the van, and I was shaking like a leaf.

That day, I had worn a blue denim coat with a red furry collar and a red hat with coloured cherries on it. I stuck out like a sore thumb. Afterwards, I thought to myself that I would never wear that outfit again. Six months or so later, on the way to the shop, I grabbed that very coat and hat from our coat stand in the hall. I went to the shop and, in there, I saw that young man who'd held a gun to my head. I know I froze, and I could feel the blood draining from my face. I'm not even sure if I bought anything, I just left the shop as quick as I could and ran home to tell my father, 'The man who held a gun to my head was in the shop!'

My father, who usually did everything by the book, knew it was too dangerous for us to report this man, so he just told me to leave it. It was a terrifying experience, though. It was the first time I had worn that coat and hat since the hold-up, and I never wore it again after that.

Eventually my father retired, and the decision was made to move. We felt dreadful moving away – we had so many friends on both sides – but the district had never been so bad and it was getting worse. I think my mother and father were just tired of windows getting smashed, and the fact that my sisters couldn't visit us safely. My parents were sad and disappointed though, obviously.

I had a good job and so my father got me a flat in the Waterside, which he painted and decorated for me. Then my parents moved to a seaside town in Northern Ireland, and I stayed here in the city and visited them at weekends. I was living on my own, paying my own bills and very independent.

When I was nineteen, I shared a flat with another girl and we were talking one night about how we could make extra money for holidays and the finer things in life. At that time, they were recruiting for the RUC Reserve and so we thought, 'Okay, we'll try that.' I thought it was very good to serve Queen and country, but to be truthful, it was the extra money that did it for me. So I applied, did the exams and interviews, and then we had to be sworn in by a justice of the peace and pledge allegiance to God and the Queen in a house down the Culmore Road.

In the very first training class, the instructor handed out photographs of some of the atrocities orchestrated by the Provisional IRA. The first photo I looked at has scarred me to this very day. It was a photo of the body of a young man, gagged and bound – and I had been at school with him. That was the first thing I saw which really hit me hard. It was then I realised that this job was actually going to be hard work – that it wasn't as simple as earning extra money.

I still had my nine-to-five job and I did the reserves work at evenings and weekends, or if there was an incident and we were called in. We were mostly sent to the Top of the Hill, but when the Troubles began to get particularly bad, we were sent to the Bog as well. I remember being in the Bogside during riots and having to get out of there. The police Land Rovers weren't bulletproof at that time, and the men all had their shields and helmets, while I had nothing. My job in the Land Rover was to use the fire extinguisher to put out any flames if a petrol bomb came through into the vehicle.

Our job as part-time reservists was to help and assist the regular police force. Women didn't go out on the beat on their own; they were always with a male. At that time, women weren't armed – but the men were. We were only taught to use the gun in case the male was shot and we were able to get his gun, but we were unarmed otherwise. That did change eventually. I left the RUC in 1992, and it was only then that they were starting to arm the females. Until then we were sitting ducks and more of a liability really, to be honest.

There was a time when loyalists turned against the RUC, too. I had moved flat and was living in a loyalist estate, and one night I got four tyres slashed by them. We were also stoned and petrol bombed out of Tullyally, and I can tell you, one side was just as vicious as the other side. One time, so-called Protestants from a Portadown band parade walked right over to me and spat in my face. Honestly – they were so bad, evil almost.

You were never stationed in your hometown if you were a regular RUC officer, but as a reservist you were, so people got to know you then. When I finished duty at night, I didn't know if the IRA would be after me, or the loyalists, because now they were out to get us, too. My flat had a dark entrance around the back and going home after finishing duty at night, I'd be praying to God, 'Please, please don't let anyone be here to shoot me tonight.' Those were real thoughts at the time …

Likewise, when the IRA started using a certain new type of drogue bomb, I remember travelling in a Land Rover under the Shipquay Street archway, thinking to myself, 'Please, God, don't let them be up above me with one of those bombs.' I was absolutely terrified. At the time, you just got on with it, and you still got up the next morning for your 'own' job. Then I'd get a phone call to work to say, 'Change your route on the way home today; we have intelligence that they are going to shoot a reservist coming from their work this afternoon.'

At 4.00am one morning the doorbell rang. I lived alone and thought, 'Who is this?' so I didn't answer it. Then I looked out the window and saw a police car driving away, so I rang them and asked what they wanted. I was told they had been coming to warn me, 'Don't answer your door to anyone because there's going to be a door-step shooting.' They actually *came* to my door to tell me not to open my door. If it wasn't so serious, it would be funny.

After that, they set me up with an alarm system, but I was a nervous wreck. If a bird flew past or a dog ran past, the alarm would go off and I would panic that someone was out there to shoot me. It made me so nervous; it was safer for me not to use it. I also had to check my car every single morning in case there were bombs under it. That was standard procedure – you never got into the car without checking it first.

I haven't ever really talked about any of this before. It's only now, when I think about some of the things we experienced, that it really hits me. I can understand why so many ex-RUC people are alcoholics today. The RUC hierarchy are fine – it was the ordinary police officers, men and women, sent out to do the dirty jobs who suffered most.

I never felt safe in the RUC, and I felt I had to keep my job a secret a lot of the time. It also depended on where you were living, too. You had to be careful about what you hung on your washing line, and you never hung your uniform out for people to see. Even when you were out at night, or went anywhere really, you were always on your guard. There was no support for us.

In April 1981, I was called to a house where a young woman was murdered on a doorstep while collecting census forms. I was terrified. The police and the army had left the scene, so there was nobody left there but the little girl who lived there and nobody to cover me if the gunmen came back. The little girl's mummy, who wasn't at home at the time, knew there was a policewoman taking care of her, but to be honest, I was only young myself. That was a scary night – being there on my own – but you didn't really question it. It was just part of the work.

I remember I was supposed to be working one night in 1976, but rang in and cancelled. That same night, a fellow female reservist was shot on Chapel Road and later died of her injuries. She was only nineteen, and the first female RUC officer to be killed here. It could so easily have been me on that beat, though. She was only a girl, and her daddy was actually shot close by two years earlier.

> When I finished duty at night, I didn't know if the IRA would be after me, or the loyalists, because now they were out to get us, too.

Occasionally, the RUC asked you to help as typists, too, and some of the things we read were unbelievable. What the terrorists didn't know about you wasn't worth knowing. They knew it all. My parents didn't like me being involved in any of that. They were supportive and didn't say too much, but I could tell they were scared, too.

We were shot at, stoned and petrol bombed in Gobnascale, both on patrol and in the Land Rover. During the riots, I had no headgear, no shields, nothing. I actually handed the guns out to the boys from the back of the Land Rover, and then got out myself with no protection.

On some Saturday mornings, we had to patrol Spencer Road in plain clothes looking for incendiary devices in shops. All we had was a walkie-talkie, we walked in and out of shops as though we were shopping, looking for anything suspicious. I always felt safer in plain clothes, because in a uniform you often felt like a sitting duck, waiting for someone to take a shot at you.

One year, I attended a language class and there was another man from the Reserves at these classes, too. He and I were called in by Special Branch one day and informed that we were being watched at the school. They said we were going to be targeted, and that they were planning to either blow us up or shoot us. That was very frightening for me.

I had a massive heart attack in 1991; three cardiac arrests in one night, and I didn't work after that. I resigned from the RUC the following year. I had been married to a military policeman from England, John, but he died of cancer after only three and a half months of marriage together. He was only twenty-six when he died. I think it was all the stress of looking after him, still working both jobs, and trying to keep the fact that he was military police a secret from everyone around us, that made me ill.

When I felt the sickness and pains that night, I still didn't imagine it was a heart attack. John had to drive me to hospital, despite him being very, very ill himself at the time. I arrested as soon as I got into the hospital. Then I arrested again twice in resuscitation, and I can remember hearing them saying, 'We're losing her … we're losing her … we've lost her.' I had an out-of-body experience, and it has played on me for such a long time since. It was horrendous. I could feel myself going up and then coming back into myself again, but it was all darkness – none of this light that people talk about. I couldn't speak, and I could hear a nurse talking into my ear the whole time, telling me it was going to be okay. I knew I'd had a heart attack, because I had watched everything from above and had seen everyone working on me, and I can remember trying to say to them, 'You must save me; I have to look after John.'

Afterwards, every time I felt a pain I panicked that it was another heart attack, but it was usually panic attacks. It was still very scary, but at least nobody has ever died of a panic attack. Doctors then told me that I could never have children because of the risk to my heart, but thankfully, I had my son years later.

John died in Altnagelvin. He was my first true love, and I am so glad that I met him and married him. He was so lovely. We made our time together count, and if I'd never met anyone else, I wouldn't have minded – I loved him so much.

I spent seventeen years in the RUC altogether, and I did feel like we made a difference sometimes. I can remember getting home from the Bogside after 4.00am some mornings, and then getting up again for my own job at 9.00am. I was much younger then, but it was still a job of some responsibility with seven staff below me.

I left the RUC in 1992, and it still wasn't safe then. I never felt safe the whole time I was there, and seventeen years was quite enough for me. Sometimes I wonder how I did the things I did. After I left the RUC, I think I had a nervous breakdown. I wasn't coping anymore, I was always nervous and I didn't want to go out anywhere or involve myself with anyone. The doctor wanted to put me on tablets but then suggested other therapies and that has helped me a lot. It gave me a reason to get up and dressed every day. I met a good friend during this time. She had me in stitches with crazy stories of hers. I laughed and laughed, and I didn't think that would have happened that first day. We have been friends since.

I never thought I would speak about these experiences, but maybe the time is right. I know too many people who now see psychiatrists because of the things they've seen in the past. I know one man, in particular, who had great difficulty walking past butchers' shops with meat hanging in the window – because of the things he saw after bombings. He had seen bodies butchered so badly by bombs, seeing meat hanging like that brought it all flooding back to him.

It's hard to think that this is such a tiny island, yet there are people doing that to each other.

Anonymous

Every time I go over that bridge, I'm back home

For centuries now, Derry/Londonderry's Fountain estate has been a proud, thriving Protestant community – the last of its kind on the city's west bank. Sadly, many families fled to safer areas as tensions escalated, and a mass redevelopment of the area saw numbers further dwindle. Local woman 'Pearl' (not her real name) lived happily in the Fountain for many years with her children and her husband, a soldier serving in the British Army. She reflects on both its heyday and darker days.

We grew up in the Fountain and it was a very happy place to live. Everyone knew each other and knew each other's business. There were no secrets, and that continues, even to this day. It's a very tight-knit community. The area belonged to families and everyone had a relation in the street. My granny and aunts were all from the Fountain before us, and so my mother's three sisters lived directly opposite us growing up.

I had three brothers and three sisters; I was the baby – a wee mistake! My mother was forty-five when she had me, and my closest sister in age is now eighty-two years old. We went to Carlisle Road Primary School and had many happy days in it. Family life was great, and as the youngest I was always spoiled. We never struggled and were well looked after. My daddy was a firefighter, and my mother worked in the shirt factory. Our back yard faced onto the old jail tower in Bishop Street, with the Long Tower and the Bogside just a stone's throw away. We were in the old houses – they are long gone now.

Bishop Street was a real community back in those days. We had a chemist, a clothes shop, a fruit shop, a butcher's shop, a bakery, Wee Johnny's shop – all close by and serving the Long Tower, too. It was sad to see that go. Anyone from the Fountain will tell you we had happy days there. We had no need to go down the town because we had everything we needed around us.

When we lived in the Fountain, we were often attacked by youths from the Bishop Street area and the street was petrol bombed and stoned. It was very scary at times, but it's hard to remember details now. There were four entrances to the Fountain alone, so as the trouble got worse, the men barricaded the street and manned it at night to control who came and went into the area.

One by one, the people all seemed to move out of the Fountain. That old sense of community was taken away and they built a lot of flats and maisonettes. My two elderly aunts were in their eighties and were rehoused in a second-floor maisonette. My aunt and uncle lived above that – three storeys up. They knocked down the old houses, and ours was demolished during the big redevelopment for the new Fountain.

Nobody helped when they were moving people out – except other families. I was twenty-four when we were rehoused. When you got word you were allocated a house, you had to move quickly, and so we moved to Victoria Street. At least we were still in the Fountain, though, and we still had all our neighbours. Well, those who stayed … Our neighbour Dorothy had lived beside us all her life and wanted to stay beside us, so we decided to wait until the next batch of houses, and kept our own neighbours. A lot of people didn't have the patience to wait for new houses and moved over to Lincoln Courts in the Waterside, which had just been finished. We sat it out, waiting for the new house. But once they built the new ones, the spirit went – it just wasn't the same.

I met my husband when I was twenty-six years old, and he was thirty-three at that time. He was from East Belfast and here as a serving soldier in the Royal Artillery Regiment when I met him. He had joined the army long before the Troubles even started. I met him in my aunt's house in the Fountain when he came in for a cup of tea – as often happened when the army first came in to do patrols. I remember I was leaving something into her house when I heard this Belfast voice telling

> He had joined the army long before the Troubles even started ... If he was worried, he didn't show it. He had served in Borneo and Malaysia before, so he was used to action.

me there was football on TV and that I was disturbing it. I won't tell you what I thought of him then! How dare he tell me I shouldn't disturb him?

I had actually met him before then, too. I always got the bus to my work in a school, and was running late one day, when a voice said on the way past, 'Are you late, love?' I told him to f*** off. It turned out that was him, too. He found out then who I was, and I suppose he took a shine to me. That's when he came to my house and asked my mother to invite him in for a cup of tea and we got to know each other. He brought her free coffee, too – and we never had coffee in the house! That sowed the seeds and led to romance. Three years later, we got married.

My husband did several tours of duty in Northern Ireland. I did worry about him, because the trouble was escalating, but if he was worried, he didn't show it. He had served in Borneo and Malaysia before, so he was used to action. He was a sergeant, so I think he was more frightened for the young men under him.

So that was love … In those days, the army weren't allowed into the city centre, so we had to get permission to allow him over this side of the river to get married in Carlisle Road Church.

After one week of married life, he was away again. I didn't travel with him. I didn't want to be an army wife, I didn't want to travel, and so we agreed that he would do his thing and I would stay here, and that worked for us. He was a man I could trust, and he could trust me, so our marriage worked very well.

I only saw him three times a year when he came home every four months, and we had two children close together. He wasn't allowed to stay at our address when he came home on two weeks' leave, but he secretly did. He just gave the army my brother's address up the road. If people knew, nobody would have said anything anyway.

Nothing bad ever happened to him or the men under him, thank God. I do remember one story about him serving in Ballymurphy in Belfast and the men were in the sangar, keeping lookout. His men pointed out someone coming in their direction, swaying from side to side, and one said, 'Sarge, there's a man coming up the street and I don't like the look of him.' My husband took the binoculars, looked out, and said, 'Hold fire, that's my da!' His father had walked miles from where they lived in Belfast to leave him up a fish supper. That really made me laugh.

Our family life was good. My husband retired from the army in 1981, after twenty-two years' service, when our youngest was two years old. That was the first child he could really help with and watch grow up, and because of that, they were very close. My son is thirty-three now, and he took it very bad when his father died.

After leaving the army my husband got a job in the Post Office, and, by that time, the city was getting worse. Everybody felt it. You never knew if you were going to be caught up in a bomb or a shooting. When we lived in the Fountain, a neighbour four doors away was shot dead on his doorstep; he was a part-time UDR man. My mother saw him coming home and a figure running, but she paid no heed to it – until she heard the bang. Another neighbour of ours was a part-time RUC man as well as a breadman, and he was shot dead one day while out delivering bread.

Because of the Troubles all around us, my children were almost used to hearing about people being shot or caught in bombs so it didn't scare them too much. It was just an everyday occurrence. Nobody seemed frightened around us. I was more frightened in Belfast if something kicked off, because I wouldn't know where to run, but we just got on with it here. It is strange how people lived through it – I think both sides of the community shut themselves off from it.

My older sister was married to an RUC man long before the Troubles ever started and they lived in Belfast where he was stationed – there was a rule that you couldn't be stationed in your own town. I was glad my husband was out of the army, but he still had that threat over him because of the army background. I think faith carried us through.

My brother was in the RUC, too, and my mother went out looking for him many a night during the Troubles when additional RUC men were drafted into the town during riots. I can still see my mother and our old neighbour Dorothy out searching the streets for him – Dorothy shuffling along behind her with no teeth in!

Normal life had to go on, though. We had no choice. My children were brought up in the Fountain, but they weren't brought up to be bitter. They had their own activities, like the Boys' Brigade and the Church, and they had a tight-knit group of friends who looked out for each other. There was nothing for the young people in the Fountain back then. At least today, there is a youth club. I think there is more bitterness today, in this generation, than there was when my boys were growing up. I feel that the young men today – on both sides – seem to have more hatred amongst them.

We loved the Fountain, but the redevelopment ruined it in a way. It took away the community spirit we loved so much. About twenty-five years ago, the rents began to get too high for us, and my husband said we might as well make the move. We could have bought my mother's house for £2,000, which was very cheap, but then we asked ourselves, who would buy it from us if we ever wanted to move again? The Troubles had started by then, and maybe nobody would want it.

It was a wrench to move to the Waterside. It broke my heart moving over here because every time I go over that bridge, I'm back home.

Absent role models

> I never saw my daddy in the coffin. When I went home, he was gone and we weren't allowed to talk about him anymore.

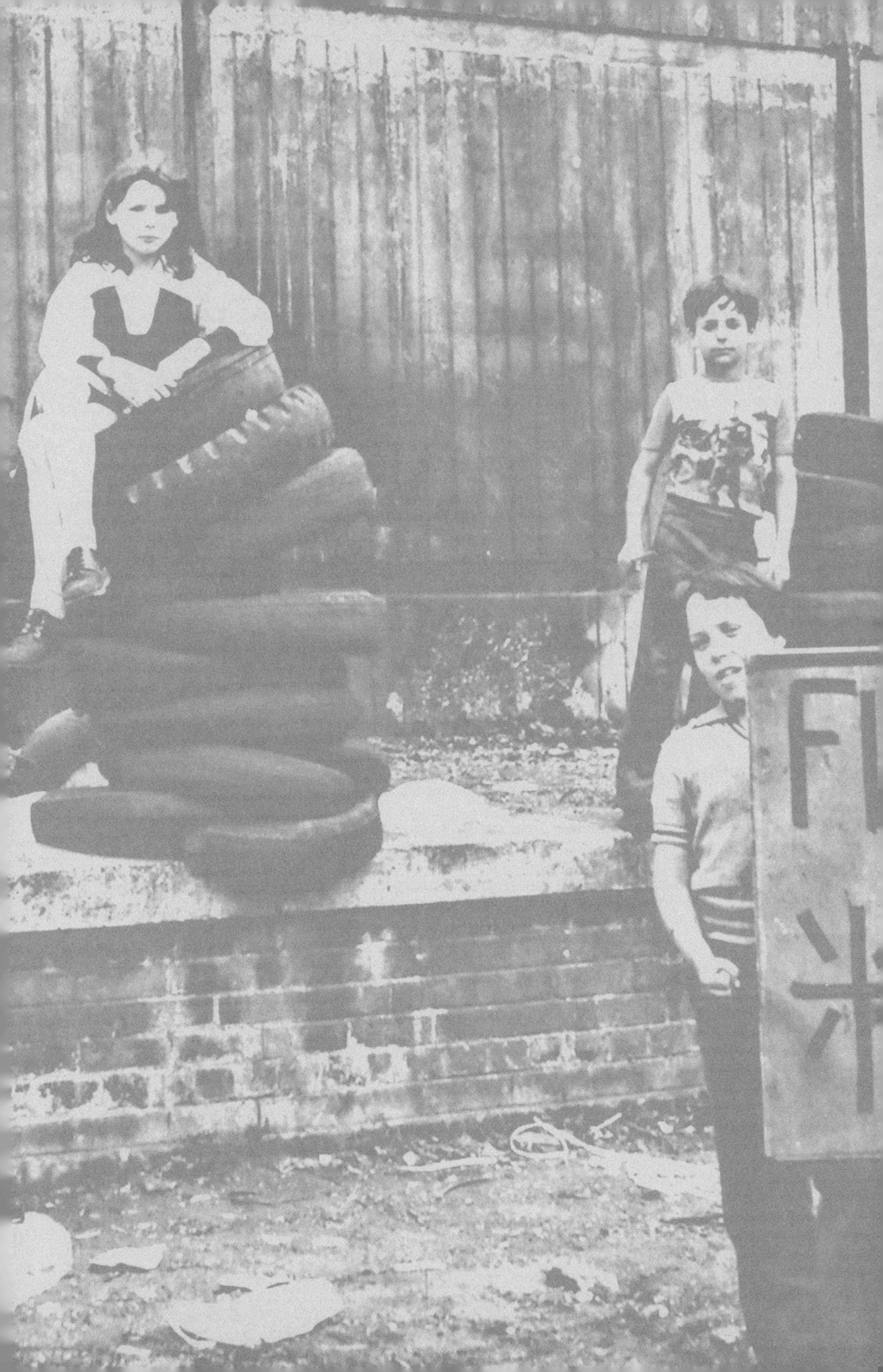

Anonymous

He was supposed to be my daddy

The voices of children often go unheard in the clamour of conflict, and for one woman, the decisions of her father – a political prisoner – had a lasting and devastating impact. 'Rebecca', who wishes to remain anonymous, reveals how her father never returned home after serving his jail sentence. Instead, he left his four children and began a new family elsewhere.

It's something I have carried all my life … My father went to jail when I was four years old, and, when you're so young, you don't understand why you have a father one day and you don't the next. You don't understand why, one day, he's home making dinner and lighting the fire, and the next, you're being dragged out of your bed with police and soldiers everywhere.

You just don't understand why – and nobody tells you. You just know he's gone, that's it. Nobody explains anything to you. The next you see of him is after a bus journey to Crumlin Road Jail. I was the youngest, so I was the one who always had to go on the weekly visits with my aunts and uncles. My sisters had started working so they couldn't go as often as they wanted. Little did we know we would spend our childhood and teenage years travelling to see him.

My mother was absent, even though she was there. She was just cold. My father was the one who gave us his time and effort. He was the one that was always around, and I have far more memories of him than her. He was like a hero to me. Especially after my mother abandoned us and was never heard from again.

I remember when I was five years old there was a buzz around the house, so we knew my father's family were visiting. We didn't know it at the time, but we were being shipped off to live with my granny. The next time I saw my mother was after my granda died, and my sister went looking for her – many, many years later. At that young age, there were a lot of nights where I cried myself to sleep because I just didn't understand what was going on. My brothers and sisters probably weren't as upset as I was because I was the youngest and probably the softer one.

My father spent over a decade inside as an IRA prisoner. It has been harder for me, because I spent all those years going to jail to support him. The family supported him, too. But then he got out of jail, and took up with another woman and had two children with her – and he was gone from our lives. That was really hard to take. I was in my early twenties when he eventually got out. He was out on parole when my first son was born, because he came to hospital to see him, and was out properly by the time I was twenty-three. Sometimes I used to wish he *had* died in the Troubles, because then at least I would have a grave to visit. To me, it feels like I mourn something that's not dead.

He never came back. He is still alive, although I hear he's not keeping the best. I did try to make contact once. I messaged him when my marriage broke down. I thought life was too short, so I contacted him and told him I felt no animosity towards him and that I hoped he was well, but nothing came back. He is in contact with some of the family, but you can't make a person do something they don't want to do.

For me, at least I know I can hold my head up high and know I never did anything wrong. I do feel sad because he has lost out on my beautiful, well-grounded children. He has also missed my sister's children, and has a great-grandchild he knows nothing about, too, but that's his loss.

> In this country, you aren't offered counselling, you get offered a tablet and told to go on home.

I don't think about my mother the way I think about him. She was gone and that was it, but it's harder when you give someone so much of your time. I cried all those years. I just wanted and wished for him to come out of prison so we could have this normal life. Then he did get out, and we never got that normal life. He had something else in mind. That's disappointing and hard to take really.

I really do feel I'm grieving for someone who's not dead, but it wasn't my fault. I was the child and they were the parents – they gave us up. I had a few tough years myself, but I couldn't imagine ever walking away from my children. As a parent, I just don't know how people can make that decision. I know I never could.

It has definitely affected how I brought up my own children, too. It made me more determined as a parent not to repeat that cycle – I would never put my children through what I went through. Should they hate me in twenty years' time because of the way I reared them, I don't care. I'll know when I go to my grave that I was always there for them. Whether it was the right or wrong decision for them throughout their lives, I was there. At night, when my children closed their eyes, I was there. When they got up in the morning, I was there. That's what a parent is supposed to do. He was supposed to be my daddy ...

You spend a lot of time fighting with yourself. In those early years, my education really suffered. I thought a lot about it all when he was gone. Wondering why, wondering when it would all stop, and why normality was robbed from us after waiting all those years. You think you know a person. I had him on a pedestal and he just left us.

When I was young I went to stay with a host family in the USA for six weeks, and I remember I didn't want to come home because, to me, that's what a family was. I didn't want to leave all that behind me. My happiest memories of being a child are those spent with that family. The host mother even got attached to my father; she really cared and spent years writing to him in jail and sending him things. She was a good friend to him, and in many ways, she was a backbone for me. She has helped me so much over the years, and it's her I talk to about most things.

My host mother comes to Ireland frequently now. If I could pick a mother, I would definitely pick her, and she knows that. She accepted us as we were. Our house was always crazy, but still she came over and she loved us regardless. None of it mattered. She has been a massive part of my life, and she has been a big part of my children's lives, too.

For a few years, I probably resented my granny because of the way we lived, but when I got older and had children myself I realised that this woman had a big family of her own and still took on another four children. How did she manage to do it? There were grandchildren living with her, too, and so I saw her with admiration. She did the best she could.

My granny had a heart of gold. She would never tell you she loved you, you just knew. My granda was quite a character, too, and looking back, I don't know how she did half of it. She never got it easy, either, and she was a saint, considering. She tried to keep us sheltered. My granny was only sixty-three when she died, and I wish now that I had asked her how she felt about it all.

My sisters rarely talk about my father or mother nowadays. They don't want to know, but I would like to talk about it. I'm not sure if that's because I'm the sentimental one. Maybe it would have helped to talk to someone about it, but in this country, you aren't offered counselling, you get offered a tablet and told to go on home. If I saw my father in the street I'd probably throw my bloody arms around him, I loved him so much. That's the worst thing about it.

When you look at it now, you wonder what it was all for. We all lived through it. It may have felt the same, and we all went through similar experiences, but our stories are totally different. So many families were destroyed, so many families lost their loved ones, and for what? It really is the pain of Ireland.

Colette O'Connor

The man with the blackthorn stick

A lone memorial is now all that remains of the Devenney family home on the edge of Derry's Bogside. Terraced townhouses lined the street back in April 1969, when RUC officers burst into the home of Sammy Devenney, savagely beating both him and his family. The father-of-nine later died of his injuries and is regarded by many as the first victim of the Troubles in Northern Ireland. One of Sammy's six daughters, Colette O'Connor (née Devenney), was just ten years old when she witnessed the attack, and today, forty-seven years on, she's still pursuing answers.

I was born in Derry in 1958, one of nine children. We grew up in 69 William Street, which is a car park today with my daddy's memorial in front of it. The Devenney family were there for generations before us and it had once been a shop and taken in lodgers, too.

One of those lodgers stayed with us and became part of our family when we moved in. His name was Harry Brown, we called him Uncle Harry. He had come in from Killea in my grandmother's time. When my granny and uncles emigrated to America, my daddy stayed here and rented the house – which still included his brother Terry and Harry the lodger. Terry eventually got married and left, but Uncle Harry stayed and was a part of our family. We loved him. He lived with us and he died with us.

I was ten around the time my daddy got battered, and I was just about to start secondary school. There were always riots erupting at the end of our street, now known as Aggro Corner, and it always seemed to be on a Saturday that trouble flared. It was very scary sometimes and you just wanted to hide under your bed. I used to lie in our back bedroom with the radio at full blast to try to drown out the noise outside from all the missiles and glass being broken, the constant roaring and the smashing of petrol bombs.

I just wanted to shut my mind off to it all. I remember one time the radio was playing The Beatles' *Give Peace a Chance* and I remember listening to it and thinking, 'I *wish* to God they would!' That still stands out in my mind. The next morning there'd be a mass of rubble, stones and glass all over the street, but by Monday morning, it would be gone, cleaned up, and it looked like it had never happened. That was strange. Then the next week it would start all over again.

The day it all happened, on 19 April 1969, I had taken my younger brother Jim to the pictures, and we could sense that some kind of trouble was starting on our way home. What was unusual that day was that my mother was in her bed sick, which didn't happen very often, and my daddy was doing the cooking. I remember he did something with bean juice to make red mash, and it was awful!

My daddy was talking to two friends at our front door and I remember peeping out to look down the street. I saw rioting down at the bottom end, so it looked like there was no danger, and then my daddy chased me in again.

I went back inside, and then suddenly the living-room door opened and it sounded like thunder in the hall. I was aware of all these bobbing heads going past in the hall and thinking, 'What's happening?' There were people running through our house. Then the police arrived at the door in their long coats and their helmets. I could see them through the net curtain. One of them looked right in the window and I think I screamed.

I remember all this commotion and my daddy shouting, 'Watch the wains!' and all of a sudden, everything was pushed into the living room. I was thrown onto a chair between my two brothers, who were eleven and six at the time. I was stuck in the middle. I couldn't see what was happening, but I could hear all sorts of roaring and a lot of bad language, them calling us everything.

Freddie, one of the neighbours who'd been talking to Daddy, lay across us on the armchair and was on top of us, screaming, 'Watch the wains, watch the wains!' When you are young, and you see a man *that* afraid, of course you're going to be terrified, too. I felt the weight of him heavy on me, and the next thing I felt was the blood coming down on me, literally pouring. They had busted his head open, and when he stood up he was drenched in blood and so was I.

Then I saw Daddy lying unconscious on the floor. I just thought, 'My daddy is dead,' because there was all this blood everywhere and coming out of his head. Our Ann was lying on top of him, crying and screaming. I saw an inspector coming in and he had a blackthorn stick in his hand. I didn't know what it meant, but I told my mother he had a blackthorn stick, and it turns out it's a symbol of rank and identifies an inspector in the RUC. He looked at me, I looked at him, and I thought he was going to whack me with the stick, instead he just looked around the room with what seemed like an expression of satisfaction, like it was a 'job well done', and then he walked out the door.

Our Cathy, who was sixteen and just out of hospital, was battered, too. She had really short hair at the time, and our Ann kept screaming, 'She's a girl!' but it didn't matter, they beat her anyway. She's never been the same since.

Men who had run into our house were still hiding upstairs in our bedroom. They were probably just as scared as we were and had nowhere to go. When I went in, they talked about me being covered in blood, wondering if I'd been hit. I kept saying, 'It's not my blood, its Freddie's blood. My father's dead.' Then Uncle Harry came upstairs and told the men to get out. When I told him my daddy's dead, he assured me he wasn't …

My sister tried to gather us up and put us all into my mammy's bed while they tried to sort things out and get an ambulance. They couldn't get the ambulance because the police stopped it coming into the street. By that stage, men from the bar across the street had come over to help.

Me, Christine and Danny were all in Mammy's bed and traumatised. We were all crying but with no tears, just noises coming out. Then something almost funny happened. Looking around, we saw a strange boy in the bed with us – we'd never seen him before! We just stared, wondering who he was, but nobody knew. He must have run in during the commotion, and he was ordered into bed with the rest of us. Honest to God, we couldn't believe it, in the middle of all that madness. We did actually laugh about that afterwards.

It seemed to get dark very quickly. When the ambulance finally arrived, I went downstairs to see the men from the bar putting my daddy into it. He put his hand out to me, but he was covered in blood so I ran away, I was terrified. Cathy and the others went over, though.

Later on, I went downstairs again and there were people in the house. I remember Eamonn McCann being there, helping to clean the place up. I asked him where my mammy was and he told me they were still in the hospital, so I went back up to my room.

The next morning it was business as usual. My mammy insisted we were going to Mass and made us get washed and dressed; I suppose we were all on autopilot. When we opened the front door to go out, it was just flash after flash, all these cameras pointing at us, and the press outside. We didn't want to go out, but my mother made us and we walked right through them and up to Mass.

My daddy got out of hospital on the Wednesday. The living room was full of people and I remember standing at the door, looking in at him sitting at the fire. His poor face – his two eyes were totally swollen, and his face, mouth and head was all battered in. I just looked over, and he looked back at me and gave me a wee wave.

The next day my daddy took a heart attack and was rushed back into hospital again. He came home after a few weeks and things were as normal as they could be, I suppose. He was scared and nervous all the time; he just wasn't the same man anymore. He was only young at forty-three, and my mum was only forty.

I suppose we had a false sense of security because Daddy seemed to be getting better. One day he took my grandparents to Buncrana and back. That same evening, he went to bed early. After a while, I went upstairs myself and the minute I hit the blankets, I heard this horrible noise – a very loud noise – like someone gasping for breath. I jumped out of the bed and, just then, my mammy started to scream and before they could get a doctor, my daddy was dead. He took a heart attack and died, very suddenly, in his own bed.

Because I was only ten, I was afraid to see him. I didn't want to see him dead. It was so shocking. It made us grow up overnight. Our Caroline was only a baby at the time, and she'd been upstairs in the cot on the day the attack happened while my mammy was beside her in bed, sick.

Two priests came to the house and gave my father the Last Rites. My mammy then asked them to take us to my granny's house in Southend Park, which they did. We all piled into the bed beside my granda. He was crying and saying the rosary, saying that he should be dead instead of my daddy. My granda had a bad heart, too, you see. I remember we were given wee tablets, I suppose they must have been sleeping tablets or something to keep us calm.

My uncle Jim and I walked down from Creggan on the day of the funeral and the hearse was outside our house. When I saw Ann and Cathy dressed all in black but looking pure white, I just started to cry. Something just came over me … I got to our door and had a panic attack, knowing that I didn't want to see my daddy in the coffin. I cried, and wouldn't go in with anyone but my mammy.

So my mammy came out to get me. She put her arms around me and brought me inside. At that point, my uncle James, my daddy's brother who lived in Birmingham all his life, came down our stairs. He was the double of my daddy and I just fell apart again. It was just like seeing my daddy …

In those days, the women didn't go to the funeral. They stayed at home while the men did the whole funeral part. Our boys all went, even the smaller ones, but we said our goodbyes in the house. I have no regrets about not seeing Daddy in the coffin.

My aunt in Creggan had sent me to the bakery a few days before, and, of course, everyone was talking about my daddy, and two women were having a conversation in the bakery about him. One said, 'What about that poor man, Devenney? I hear they're cutting him up to see what happened to him.' At ten years of age, I already knew what a post-mortem was because my mum had just explained that to us, but to use the term 'cutting him up', that really got to me. My cousin told me to wait outside … I know we're only human, and we're all guilty of saying the wrong things at the wrong time, but I think all that talk probably made me more afraid of seeing my father in the coffin.

We coped because my mammy was such a strong person really. She had tablets that the doctor had given her, but she threw them in the fire after the funeral. Thank God she did, too, because God knows where we would have ended up if she'd relied on tablets.

As we tried to get back to normal, the rioting was a constant reminder of what had happened, so we went to stay with relatives on a farm in Ballybofey for a few days before 12 August. My sister Ann and my older brother Harry stayed in Derry, but the rest of us were delighted to get away. The farm was a great environment for us, because we were able to fix hay and help the woman next door take cows for milking. It was great. We didn't need much with us, so I had the dress I was wearing, another for Sunday and a change of underwear. That was it.

While we were there, the grown-ups were watching the riots in Derry on the TV news when they saw our house totally demolished. They had set fire to Richie's factory next door, and it fell in on top of our house, destroying it. We never went back into it again. What bothered us most was all my daddy's things being in there. We wanted our reminders of him more than anything else. We did manage to get photographs out of the rubble, but the wall had fallen in, and a lot of things had already been looted. That was just a month after he was buried.

We had nowhere else to go, so from Ballybofey we went to Buncrana and stayed in a caravan site for the first night. We had no choice. The next day, I was in a field in Buncrana when a woman called me over. I thought, 'Who's she talking to?' but I went over and she said, 'You're one of the Devenneys, aren't you?' I said yes, and she brought me into her house, and up to her daughter's wardrobe, and started handing me clothes and pillows and blankets, things to help us out. People were so good to us.

After the caravan, my mother rented a flat in Main Street in Buncrana. Then Dr MacDermott, a good friend of my mammy's, came to see us and said, 'Phyllis, there's a house over the street. We're planning to move back up to Derry, so you take it for as long as you need it.' He was so good to my mammy, and so we moved in there until we were housed in Derry.

We moved back to Derry when I was starting St Mary's Secondary School that September. We got a house in Shantallow, and then my mother did a swap for a house in Cable Street. When I started school, the nuns took me into a room and gave me a uniform. Everybody weighed in to help us at that time. Something like that changes your perception of material things. You don't give a damn about stuff, it's not important.

After my daddy died, there was huge political upheaval but no solution to his case. Even now, all these years later, there is still no solution to it. My mother always thought that someone would come forward and admit what they did – that their conscience would eventually bother them. No-one ever did, though, and to be honest, I don't think they ever will. So I have to make them … I have to keep at it, and force something to happen. I can't just sit around and do nothing.

There is information out there. The Metropolitan Police are holding files from the Drury Report. Kenneth Drury came over from Scotland Yard to investigate my daddy's case in 1969. He gave twelve copies of his report to the RUC but, unbelievably, we have never seen it. My mother died having never seen it, even though it was the only inquiry ever carried out into my daddy's case.

Through the Pat Finucane Centre, we approached the Police Ombudsman Nuala O'Loan to take on our case. She said they would need new evidence before she could start any new investigation, and there *was* evidence that hadn't been mentioned before – *my* evidence. I'd seen the man with the blackthorn stick, and that particular fact had never been mentioned before. We witnessed everything, but had never been properly interviewed. You could hardly call that a real investigation, could you? She agreed to look into it.

> My mother always thought that someone would come forward and admit what they did – that their conscience would eventually bother them. No-one ever did, though, and to be honest, I don't think they ever will. So I have to make them … I can't just sit around and do nothing.

It's unbelievable that we had no access to the only report they ever did. Whenever Nuala O'Loan went looking for the Drury Report in 2001, she found out that the Metropolitan Police had one copy. She got it and concluded that my daddy wasn't murdered and he had a bad heart. Even if he did, they still had no right to batter him. They still broke the law. She said that because there was an amnesty in 1969, the RUC were protected and nobody would ever go to court for it.

We still don't have a copy of the original report, but we have a copy of *her* report into that first report. In hers she recounted my daddy's last day, and that was very sad for us. She cried when giving us that report. To be honest, I think she cried because her hands were tied, and she knew she was giving us a bum steer. I think, in her position, she had no choice.

We're still fighting to see the Drury Report – just to see it. The Pat Finucane Centre discovered that this file was briefly opened at The National Archives in Kew last year, but they closed it again as it 'wasn't in the public interest'. We're still trying …

I'm insulted that they still want to protect the RUC after all these years. Where is the duty of care to us? We have no closure. We never got our day in court. For me, personally, I can't *not* do something. When the Pat Finucane Centre approached us about the files in Kew – I knew we had to try. God knows what's over there. Look how much they've found in those files in recent years.

I always think about my mammy. How must it have been for her? She lost her partner and had nobody. It must have been terrifying. My mother was such an important person in our lives. I was young when my daddy died, and so she was our mother and our father for all those years. When she died at sixty-four, we were heartbroken, but at least we were able to grieve for her death, and reflect, and think about her in happier times. People still stop me in the street and tell me little stories about her.

My daddy was different, because there was no closure and we couldn't grieve. It's still too painful because nothing has ever been explained. It annoys me that people – politicians – think you can brush things under the carpet. You can't. Sometimes things are just too raw and too painful to forget. Too many people here need answers, and that should be made a priority. We can't move forward until this is addressed, for everybody. In terms of my daddy's case, this has to end with us. It's a fear I have, I don't want to pass any burden on to my children. I want this sorted out in our lifetime; we can't leave it for another generation.

It's important to talk about these things now – it's therapeutic. Especially if you feel your voice hasn't been heard. People need to know the real history from those who lived it, and we shouldn't be afraid to talk.

I became a grandmother recently, and my sister Ann said to me at the time, 'Can you imagine – Daddy never saw any of us get married, never walked any of us up the aisle, never saw any of our children being born – his own grandchildren.' We often talk about him like that. My daddy was very much a family man and he loved Christmas and holidays. When he was cooking Christmas dinner, he used to chase after us with the turkey feet!

My parents were such a great couple; they had their dreams and talked of us visiting America. He missed out on all of that … I suppose we all did.

Christine Robson

The hearth was filled with my daddy's blood

Nine children lost their father when Derry man Sammy Devenney suffered a horrific beating from the RUC in 1969. Christine Robson (née Devenney) was another of Sammy's six daughters, and younger than Colette when their lives were torn apart.

I was nine when it happened and I remember it was a really sunny day outside. Every Saturday there were riots, and there was chaos in the street so we weren't allowed out the door. My father was cooking the day's dinner for the first time in his life and he mixed beans and milk for tea – don't ask me why!

The riot seemed to be all around us. You could hear it at the bottom of the street, hear it at the top of the street. It was like a no-go area with stones, bottles, all the usual. The rioting became commonplace from 1968 onwards, and it is a terrible thing to say, but I think we almost got used to it. It just became a way of living for us.

My mother knew there would be riots every Saturday night, so that was our bath night. She would bring out the big bath and we'd all get a bath for Mass in front of the fire. I was the third youngest of the nine children, and I can still see us being taken out into the yard one by one, in our vests, to get our hair combed. It was like a conveyer belt.

Sometimes we could hear the banging and noise outside, which was very scary, but you just blocked that part of your life out. We just amused ourselves with toys and TV and accepted that we weren't allowed out. That day, I was upstairs in my mammy's room playing with Caroline in the cot when I heard three big thuds and the house almost shook. Mammy said, 'What's that?' So I went to look out the window because the front door was directly underneath us.

I looked down and said, 'Mammy, men with big black coats are trying to break into our house!' They were running at our door with a big block of wood. I didn't know what a battering ram was at that age – it just looked to me like a big tree. She didn't believe me, and she told me to sit down and be quiet.

Suddenly, there was a lot of roaring and screaming. In my head, this next part feels like flashes in a film, like scenes flashing past – boom-boom-boom – all hectic. When I try to figure it out in my head, it comes in these flashes.

We had heard all the screaming downstairs, and I remember that my mammy's fear made me worse; I didn't want my mammy to be afraid. The bedroom door was closed, and my mammy was looking at me as if trying to reassure me, but she couldn't because of the chaos downstairs. For a minute, she just froze, distracted, fixing around the cot and saying, 'Don't let anyone touch the baby.'

I wanted her to go downstairs, to check what was happening, but we were both too scared. I knew she was worried. Then all of a sudden, two men burst into the bedroom and jumped into the wardrobe. They didn't even speak to us; they just jumped in there while the police came in downstairs and started beating the hell out of everybody.

I see it in flashes: they jumped in the wardrobe, there was bedlam, and we jumped up to leave the room. Then our Ann's fella came to the door and started pushing my mother back into the bedroom against her will, telling her, 'You can't go downstairs, Phyllis, you have to stay here!' While he was pushing her inside, he started pulling all the sheets and pillowcases off the bed and throwing them out on the landing, which I thought was strange. Obviously, they were to wrap around my daddy ...

It still really frustrates me to think about how those people held my mother back, and the frustration she must have felt. The fear she had. It must have been terrible. Even now, it makes me so angry thinking about it, and I crack up if someone tries to restrain or hold me back. I know they were holding her back for her own good, but maybe they should have let her go downstairs. That was *her* house. I think it was twenty minutes before they actually let her out.

My daddy fixed TVs, and that day, two men had come to collect their TVs – Freddie and Paddy. They were at the door talking when the police arrived, and they all ran inside and closed the doors to protect everyone. Those two men got as bad a hiding as my daddy did. He died, but they were badly beaten, too.

Freddie made it into the living room and threw himself on top of a couple of the wains to save them from being battered – and they beat him senseless. Paddy was beaten in the hall. My mother saw him being dragged out, and she said his face was unrecognisable. It haunted her forever – they'd beaten his face to a pulp.

My father was very strong. He fought the first policeman off, then two came at him, then more kept coming, and our Harry said there were eight policemen on him in the end, all battering him.

My next flash is sitting on the end of the bed, shaking. I was one of the lucky ones who stayed upstairs. When we were up there, Colette, Jim and Danny came into the room covered in blood, so we went hysterical. We thought they were beaten up.

The hearth was filled with my daddy's blood

In the distance, I heard people in the house saying, 'Sammy's dead,' and I went mad. 'My daddy's dead? Who killed him? What happened?' They must have thought he was dead at the time. The house was in chaos, people everywhere. The only reason the police left was because my brother Harry took a breadknife to them.

Loads of reporters were staying in the City Hotel that day because there'd been a march and it'd been a day of unrest anyway. The minute the police entered our house the reporters knew about it and made their way over. Mary Holland was the first reporter on the scene, then Bernadette Devlin came, and Dr Raymond McClean arrived, too, and came upstairs with his doctor's bag. He was a great friend to us over the years.

I didn't see what happened downstairs, but I just know it was really bad. We had a fireplace, and I remember the hearth was filled with my daddy's blood. Everyone was horrified about it. I remember people trying to mop that up, and they couldn't. It was a river of blood. There was blood on the walls, too, and I think that's why all the people were trying to clean it up, because we were so young.

My daddy was lying on the living-room floor with blood everywhere. They had beaten his false teeth down his throat and he choked on them. My sister Ann, who was the oldest at eighteen, gave him the Last Rites. She lay on top of him and said he was dead, but someone got the teeth out of his throat, and he came round again, thank God.

The police had hit him so hard, the bottom of his glasses were actually embedded into his cheekbones. He was in such a bad state and he needed a line of stitches below each eye. Ann was battered, too, and they gave our Cathy a terrible beating, even though she wasn't long sixteen and only out of hospital with a burst appendix. They hit her so hard, her new scar burst open, and she needed an ambulance, too. She's still not well today.

The police wouldn't let my brother Harry out to phone an ambulance or get help, so he went out the back and jumped over the roofs of houses on William Street to get to the parochial house. He told the priest we needed an ambulance and he phoned for one, and then three priests arrived at our door in no time, too. We were on the bed, crying our eyes out. Danny and Jim were dripping with blood, and Jim was only about six years old then. It was bedlam. Someone was asking Colette if she was cut because she was covered in blood, too. People checked all over her, and she was telling them, 'It's not my blood.'

When we were all cleaned up, we still weren't allowed downstairs until Granny and Granda came to get us. Then they took us downstairs and straight out the front door with blankets over our heads, so we couldn't see around us. We were taken to their house, and we weren't allowed to talk about it. My grandparents didn't really know what to say to us, either, but they got us lemonade and biscuits and we all shared a big bed that night. My granda looked after us and put on a brave face, but that night I heard him in his bed, breaking his heart, crying. They thought we were sleeping, but I heard him.

The next day, nobody was telling us anything, so we were guessing ourselves. I kept telling our Colette, 'He's dead.' It was very hard. Our big brother and sister, Harry and Ann, looked after us while he was in hospital, and my mammy stayed over there with him – but I just wanted my mammy and daddy. I wanted us to be what we were before all this happened.

I remember going back to the house a few days later and it was awful. There was a big hole in the front door where they broke in, the locks still weren't fixed, and for weeks afterwards, reporters were at our door constantly. We never got any peace.

I couldn't eat a bite. I knew I had to drink, so I did, but I don't remember eating food during all that time. I felt I would vomit if I ate, and I don't know how I didn't fade away. It seemed to go on for weeks and weeks. Now that I'm an adult, I realise what shock is, and I see now that we were probably all in shock.

My mother wouldn't talk about it and acted as though it didn't happen, which was her way of dealing with it. We tried to get our lives back to normal while my daddy was in hospital, but the house never emptied with people wanting to help. We did settle down a bit, but it was hard because the door was still broken and some of the blood was still on the walls.

We were excited when my daddy came home from hospital, but I was so shocked when he came in. He was bruised all over, and still had all the stitches and scars all over his head. He was frail and quiet. It was terrible seeing him so sick. I thought he was going to be the same man, but he wasn't. He was like an ox, a strong, great man, and to see him like that … he just wasn't my daddy.

The day he died was a summer's day, and he had only been out of hospital a couple of days. He had taken my granny, granda and mammy away for the day, and I remember they brought us back bars of rock from Buncrana so we were delighted.

Later, my mother was putting the wains to bed, and I was on the sofa with a sore belly. My daddy had gone to bed early, and when my mammy went up to check on him, she found him in bed having a heart attack. We heard her

The hearth was filled with my daddy's blood

screaming, and she shouted to our Danny to get an ambulance. Instead, he ran for a doctor across the street. But by the time the doctor came over, my daddy was dead. I knew he was dead. My mammy kept shouting, 'Your da's dead … your da's dead …' This time, I knew it was true, although I was only nine and didn't really grasp what dead meant.

Our Harry and Ann were at a dance at the Embassy, so I asked Danny to go keep an eye out for them. When he saw Harry coming up the street, he ran to him squealing that my daddy was dead and Harry wouldn't believe him. By the time he got up to the house, the ambulance was there with its blue flashing light.

On our landing, my mammy was walking up and down with a pair of rosary beads, crying and praying. I peeped in the crack in the door and saw my daddy lying there in the bed, dead. Then my mammy's family, the McDaids, arrived, and we were all shipped out again. We knew this time that it was for the long haul. There were piles of clothes laid out on the bed and we were being split up to stay with various relatives. This time nobody even talked, there was just a terrible wailing and crying around us.

> My daddy was dead one minute and the next minute, we lost our house, too. I think that was the worst thing of all, every memory of my daddy gone … That was just heartbreaking.

My sister Mena and I went to my aunt Moya's house in Broadway. On the way there, we were whispering to each other, 'What are we going to do now?' because we knew he was dead. We hardly slept that night. When we got up in the morning, I opened my eyes to see a hostess trolley sitting there with a whole fry on it – and it was still roasting hot. We couldn't believe it … in our house, you stood in line and were lucky to get your food! Moya was very good to us, and she had hot, running water, too, and that was great because we didn't have a bath in our house. Sometimes my mammy would have given us a shilling to go up to the City Baths and get a bath for Mass on Sunday.

When we met Moya's wains there was just silence. We hardly spoke to each other. They didn't put the TV on, I suppose out of respect for my daddy, so it was very quiet in the house. We were pining for home, and eventually Mena got her way and went back home, but I stayed. Mena was allowed to see the funeral off at the house, too, but I was too young and I stayed with my aunt.

I never saw my daddy in the coffin. When I went home, he was gone and we weren't allowed to talk about him anymore. We whispered to each other for a while and then, after a few weeks, we put the radio back on, and then after a while, the TV went back on, too.

My mammy was so sad, but she still fulfilled her role as a mother and looked after us. I think the children kept her going. To us, she was our mammy and she was going to fix it for us. When my daddy died, I pretended to myself that he was away working and would come back. I had to do that to get myself over it, because my mammy was acting as though he wasn't really dead.

The rioting had escalated in Derry because my father had died, and now it was coming up to 12 August when the Apprentice Boys paraded through the city, too, so we were advised to leave town before it kicked off. My mother didn't want to go, but my granda told us we were going to stay with relatives on a farm in Ballybofey. We did protest, but my granda had the last word and he was the boss, so off we went to Ballybofey. Only our Harry and Ann stayed behind for their jobs.

The people who owned the farm were lovely – the nicest people you ever met. It was there that we first heard children cursing and saying, 'Git de fuck,' which we thought was brilliant. We didn't curse at all. The farm was a great escape for us. Every few days, my mother would go and find a phone, and phone our Harry in Derry to check if the house was okay, and Harry would be waiting by the phone in a friend's house to take the call.

Harry and Ann were at work in Derry the day rioters set fire to Richie's factory. It caved in, crushing our house, too. My mother was making scones and watching TV when she saw her own house burning on the TV screen. They'd been filming the riots and when the camera swung around, you could see our house burning and others, too. She saw our Harry standing outside the house, powerless to do anything. So all hell broke loose, and every possession we had was gone. My mother packed up and returned to Derry, where she met our Harry at the bottom of William Street, and they stood there together, watching the house burning.

My daddy was dead one minute and the next minute, we lost our house, too. I think that was the worst thing of all, every memory of my daddy gone. I don't know how my mother coped with it all really. It was bad enough he got the hiding and died, but then to lose our home and all his things, too, less than a month later? That was just heartbreaking to us.

The Devenneys who had moved to America took my daddy's death very badly, too. They had lost their brother. We visited my father's brother in

The hearth was filled with my daddy's blood

America once, and he had a theory that the house was burned to destroy the evidence. That was all the evidence my mammy had – the house and the bloodstains on the walls. We had photos of my daddy's injuries, too, which were apparently awful. Our youngest, Caroline, found them in a cupboard when she was young, and it shocked my mammy so much that she burnt them all. That was more evidence gone, and there are no copies.

From Ballybofey, we moved to a house in Buncrana owned by Dr MacDermott, and he let us live there without taking a penny's rent from my mother. He brought us down a box of groceries every week, too. My mother was forever in his debt, they were so good to us for those six months. We eventually got a house in Shantallow and then swapped to Cable Street, which is still our family home now. We got on with our lives and tried to deal with the fallout from it all. My mother was brilliant, but I wish I had been able to talk about it to her more.

I used to ask her if she missed my daddy, and she did. Especially in later life, she said. She missed him for walks on the beach and things like that. I tried to draw it out of her and make her talk about him, but it rarely worked. She couldn't deal with our tears, and I see why she couldn't. She just blocked it out. When we all grew up, we wanted to do something about my daddy's case, and my mother told us we could do whatever we wanted, but just not to talk to her about it. She refused to discuss it.

I suppose we learned to deal with everything over the years, and today I'm happily married with a family and I have a great life. We are in an awkward place now, though. My sister Colette is trying to investigate my father's case – she needs to do it. The others don't want to pursue it, but Colette has to see this through, for herself.

I will support my sister, but I don't think we're going to get closure. I'm not sure if I want to know any more about it, but I do hope she finds what she needs. For me, it's over forty years on, and I know my daddy's not coming back. I just have to get on with my life now.

Lost Siblings

I have seen people throughout my life who have lost parents or siblings, and I have never seen a mother grieve the way my mother did.

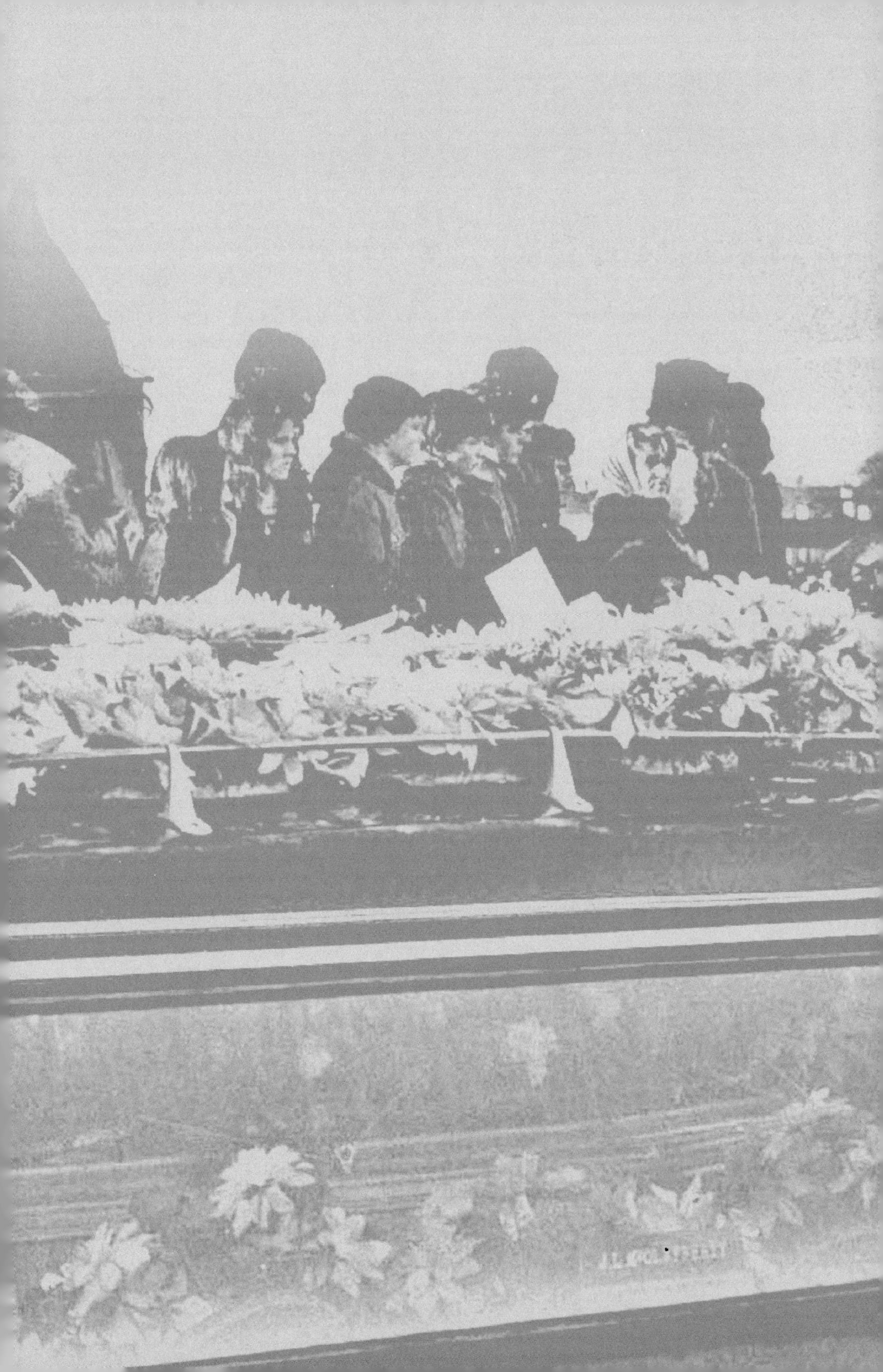

Sharon Austin

We didn't exist after my brother died

Decades after the murder of her brother in 1974, Londonderry woman Sharon Austin still struggles to comprehend the effect that this sudden bereavement had on her entire family. For the first time, Sharon reflects on her late brother and explains how his traumatic death changed everything.

I was eleven when my brother was murdered. His name was Leonard Winston Cross, and he was only eighteen years old and a happy-go-lucky teenage boy. He was flirty and funny and did anything for laughs.

Winston worked as a painter in Ebrington Barracks and was leaving his work one Friday in 1974 to join the army the following week. He had papers to sign up on Tuesday 11 November 1974 – Poppy Day – which is why that day is very significant to us. That's his day.

When he didn't come home that Friday night, my mother presumed he had gone out for a drink with friends. His best friend, Joseph 'Bert' Slater, was with him. They never came home. At first, my mother didn't worry, but she got anxious when he still didn't appear the next day. It was out of character for him to stay out all night. When my mother went to the police, they laughed at her and sent her home. They said Winston was probably away with some woman.

My mother, father and my brother Robin, who was then nineteen, went to Fort George that Sunday, and the army locked them in a hut to wait. They said they'd be back in a minute, but then they left them in there for a couple of hours, before making a laugh of them and sending them home. We believe now that the army already knew Winston and Bert were taken away.

The IRA had abducted both of them from a bar across the border. They had taken a taxi to Donegal after drinking in the Waterside. Then they went into a bar and were never seen again.

On Monday, we went to school as normal. I was at Templemore Secondary School in the Glen. On Monday night, my parents and Robin went out looking for him again, and I remember that my brother Harry, who is nearest to me in age, said, 'I don't know why they're looking for our Winston – he's dead.' He was only a child then and knew nothing, but I clearly remember he said that.

We didn't exist after my brother died

On Tuesday, my friend and I walked past two girls in the playground and I heard one of them saying, 'The police are up at the Crosses' house.' Then they saw me and walked away. We were sent home a while later.

My mother heard the news when she went into the mobile shop that drove around the Glen. She was in for cigarettes when a neighbour of ours told the shopkeeper that two bodies had been found up on Sheriff's Mountain. My mother knew it was Winston and Bert. Nobody told her – she just knew. That's how she found out …

My father took Robin and an uncle of ours to identify Winston, and it was him. Bert Slater's parents were both dead by then, so I think his only brother identified him. At least I can thank God for that part – that his parents were spared that heartache.

They had been taken to Donegal and tortured for three days before being hooded and shot on Sheriff's Mountain. There they left them – lying at the side of the road – with black bin bags over their heads. At first, the IRA said that he was an informer for the military because he worked in Ebrington Barracks. They then changed their story and claimed it was a case of mistaken identity, and they apologised for taking him and shooting him. That part is hard to take. I still have the newspaper clippings from 1974; my mother kept them all.

We were shipped out when we found out about Winston. A woman up the street kept me, and an aunt took the others, although I'm not sure how long we stayed away. Robin stayed in the house to help my mother and father sort things out. We were brought home before Winston was buried so we could see him if we wanted to. I remember I kissed him on the forehead and wondered about a mark on his face. I didn't realise at the time, but that was the bullet hole where he'd been shot.

Later, we discovered that a row had broken out in the bar in Donegal, and, while Winston and Bert weren't involved in the row, it's thought that the fight was deliberately set up to draw them outside. From there, they were taken away and tortured.

Before we went back to school, I remember my father telling us, 'Remember – Catholics did not do this. It was an organisation. It wasn't the ordinary Catholic people.' I knew that already, because it was the ordinary Catholic people who helped us bury Winston, who paid for his burial because we had no money. We had nothing. The people in the Glen were all mixed, but they still gathered together and paid for the funeral. That's how close-knit our community was.

My mother couldn't live there anymore, though. From where we lived, the house looked right out onto the TV mast on Sheriff's Mountain, and she couldn't cope with that, so her brother and sister helped us move closer to her family in town. That's where our life changed drastically.

My brother was gone, but what about the aftermath? I keep saying this to people, and nobody understands. Nobody ever came to ask us how we were, or what life was like for us after he was murdered. Life was dreadful after Winston. My parents got no support when he died, and from that day on, we had a terrible, terrible life.

My father became an abusive alcoholic. He was a sergeant major and, although he was a drinker, it was never to that extreme. Now he drank six nights a week and got very abusive and violent towards my mother and brothers. It was awful. Sunday was the only day that pubs didn't open, so I would always wake up feeling so relieved on Sundays. Then it would be Monday, and the drinking and violence would start again.

When I was a child and a row broke out, my natural instinct was to run. I didn't care if they killed each other, I just wanted to run. He never hit me – I was the only girl. But my mother worked twelve-hour shifts as a cleaner, and one morning I saw my father beating her face off a mirror before she went to work. It was so vicious, and that violence went on long after we left home. Once, he held a knife to my mother's throat, too. He didn't ever justify or explain himself, but sometimes afterwards, he would sit up the stairs crying.

My mother became totally dependent on drugs and tried to commit suicide. She tried everything to end her world. We didn't matter anymore. There was nobody else in her mind but Winston, and she could be quite violent and argumentative, too. She attended the local psychiatric hospital, and was talked to about electric-shock treatment because she kept trying to commit suicide. She must have tried at least twenty or thirty times. Once, she set the bedroom on fire to kill herself. I remember walking into the bedroom and seeing her just standing there, squealing so loud, and then fighting with me for trying to help her. She took overdoses for years, too, all when I was still a child.

I was the youngest and the only girl, which made things harder for me. My mother depended more on me, not just because I was her daughter, but because I was a girl. I played hockey for Derry for twenty years, and my mother never saw me with a hockey stick in my life. She just wasn't interested.

My parents stayed together, and my father still drank, up until the day he died. He became less abusive, and my brother says it was because they grew big enough to stand up to him, but I would honestly say I was the only person who ever stood up to him – and I'm not proud of it. When sober, my father was a gentleman – the world's best. He was just a nasty, nasty drunk.

Part of all this, I believe, was because my father came from a Catholic background and had changed his religion to Church of Ireland to marry my mother. He wasn't forced to, he chose to do it, but then after Winston was murdered, my mother was constantly angry with him. She blamed him in a way, and would say things like, 'Maybe it was one of your crowd who killed our Winston.' That was the only way she could get at someone, and so my father bore the brunt of it continuously.

My childhood was horrific. I could have disappeared off to anywhere and nobody would have noticed me gone. I was up the back lane drinking bottles of Mundies wine at the age of thirteen. Nobody knew. We went through every day, through school, came home, and nobody gave a damn.

I don't blame my father for how he turned out. I blame the circumstances. Doctors came and gave my mother Diazepam, sleeping tablets, nerve tablets, injections, and my father was left sitting in the corner. People thought, 'Ah, you don't need anything, you're a man.' He was never once asked if he needed any help, so he turned to the drink.

> My childhood was horrific ... I was up the back lane drinking bottles of Mundies wine at the age of thirteen. Nobody knew. We went through every day, through school, came home, and nobody gave a damn.

From an early age, if there was a row in the house I'd be summoned to sort it out. I was only a child – too young – but it was still, 'Get Sharon. She'll pacify him, he'll listen to her.' We didn't exist as children anymore. I wasn't classed as a child anymore. As years passed and we got older and left home, my parents would still ring me when they were rowing. No matter where I was, or what I was doing.

Yet when I was young and went into the hospital to have my appendix out – nobody came to collect me after the operation to take me home. I was left sitting there. In the end, my oldest brother and his wife came to get me. I used to think to myself, 'Children in homes would be better looked after than me.'

I love my uncle Dessie to bits, and I used to wish he were my daddy. Although they were brothers, they were completely different. Dessie wasn't violent, whereas we used to describe my daddy as, 'an outside gentleman, an inside Hyde'.

Nobody knew what went on in our house growing up. I was a child and left to my own devices. I could do what I wanted. Nobody cared. I lay on my bed every day and cried. In fact, I never had a day where I didn't lie there and cry. On the day of my father's funeral, we were standing at the front door when my uncle Dessie put his arms around me, and said, 'I love you, doll.' I was bowled over – I had waited all my life for my father to do that, and my uncle Dessie did it. It was lovely.

My eldest brother would have dealt with a lot more at home, but fortunately for him, he got married and left the house within two years. I was there until I was almost nineteen, but every one of us eventually got married. If you wanted out in those days, you had to get married.

No-one was ever charged with Winston and Bert's murders. My father went to his grave without seeing someone charged, and it was all he wanted. I still miss Winston, but there is no bitterness against ordinary Catholic people. I am very bitter and angry against the republican movement, though, and the loyalist movement, too, I have to say. I don't care who knows it, either. I have staunch loyalist friends myself, but sorry, I have to be honest.

My father was an ex-British soldier, and Winston was joining the British Army, too, but, in my opinion, I feel he would still be alive if Bloody Sunday hadn't happened here. The IRA swelled after that.

Every Poppy Day, we lay a wreath at the cenotaph in the Diamond for Winston, but we wanted to do something special for his 40th anniversary. I had this idea about letting off lanterns at his grave, so we mentioned it on Facebook to see if anyone was interested in coming along. My mother often worried that nobody remembered Winston, so we wanted to surprise her. We ended up organising a piper, poppies and lanterns for the grave. We told my mother to dress up nice so we could get a photograph taken, but she had no idea that people were coming from far and wide to remember Winston.

When we reached the cemetery, we had instructed everyone to stay in their cars until my mother reached the grave. When she got up there, all of a sudden people started coming from everywhere. All these people walking towards us – it was beautiful to see.

My mother was so blown away that she started to cry and needed help to stand up. 'Why are they all here?' she asked. 'You thought nobody remembered our Winston,' I told her. 'Look around you.' There were people there who we hadn't seen in years, old school friends of Winston's, old neighbours, friends, family members, newspaper reporters. After a minute's silence, a piper played and we released the lanterns into the sky. And, do you know, my mother's lantern floated straight towards Sheriff's Mountain …

I cried all the time until about ten years ago, when I went for counselling after my father died. It wasn't about him – it was about my own issues. I realised I needed help. I had counselling for two years.

One time, I left the Glen on Hallowe'en night and went all the way over to a party in the Waterside. I wasn't even thirteen. Nobody ever asked where I was or where I was going. Who cared? Jesus, life was tough. I used to hang around outside the off-licences until someone bought me drink. My mother didn't notice.

I literally don't remember a good day. I got married when I was eighteen and I had my daughter at nineteen. That was all I ever wanted, a baby, someone I could hold and tell them I loved them. My marriage didn't work out, I knew I didn't want to be with him. I had my second child at twenty-three and then I met Robert when my second baby was only eight months old. We are thirty years together now. When I met him, I felt real love for the first time. He shows me all the love that my parents never did. He is the love of my life, in every way.

I have seen people throughout my life who have lost parents or siblings, and I have never seen a mother grieve the way my mother did. She went to pieces. We still have Winston's clothes, you know. For over four decades, she has kept the last clothes he took off that day. She took them out before his last anniversary, and asked me to smell them, 'Do you smell Winston?' and I had to pretend I could still smell him. I didn't smell a thing …

I know in those days parents didn't tell you they loved you, but I swore when I left the house that if I ever had children, I would tell them I loved them every day of their life. We have always done that, and still do. We bring our problems to the table and we talk about it and support each other. That was the problem in our house – nobody got support after my brother died. There was nothing and nobody. My whole life I have been the mother of that family, and it's too late to change that now.

Ursula Duddy

My big brother was a pencil sketch that hung in our living room

For those born during the conflict in Northern Ireland, being part of the new generation had both its advantages and disadvantages. Ursula Duddy (née Gallagher) was born in 1976 and, while she was too young to comprehend the turmoil tearing the North apart, she was robbed of a big brother when just six weeks old. Jim Gallagher was shot dead by the British Army in May 1976, five days before his twenty-first birthday.

I'm the youngest of a big family of six girls and two boys. All my siblings are considerably older than I am, and there's a seven-and-a-half-year gap between my closest sister Fiona and me – they saved the best until last! The eldest of us was my brother Jim, who would be twenty-one years older than me.

I was born and reared in Galliagh, but my family were from Creggan Heights. At one stage, they lived in the Waterside, too, and they used to get a hard time because they were one of the few Catholics living in Shearwater Way. When the older ones talk about their childhood, they tell me about the windows being smashed in continually. My mother and father were very proud people and refused to put iron grills on the windows, so every time they got them replaced, they were broken again in a matter of days.

My sisters remember my mother and father gathering all the youngest into the kitchen when the windows were being smashed, and how they pulled out the washing machine to hide them behind it when the stones and bricks were flying into the house. Marie, my eldest sister, said the bricks would bounce into the living room and right out as far as the kitchen, and they would all be hiding in the kitchen trying to protect the children. They had hard times. My sister Fiona remembers the bricks flying into the house and hiding in the kitchen. She was the baby back then, so she would definitely have been put in behind the washing machine for safety.

When they left the Waterside, they moved to Brookdale Park in Galliagh, where I was born and grew up, and my mother lived there until she died. I feel that I lived through the tail end of the Troubles, but because of what happened in our house, I felt the sorrow of the Troubles that others my age might not have understood.

My big brother was a pencil sketch that hung in our living room

I look at my own children now growing up and they are so blissfully unaware of what it used to be like here. They are so far removed from thinking I had a brother shot dead during the Troubles – they can't wrap their head around it. When I tell them my own memories of soldiers on the street with guns and being stopped and searched if you were going up the town or going through checkpoints to get to Buncrana, they just think it's madness. It is amazing that our children don't have to live with the tensions we did. Still, I knew nothing compared to the older ones in our house. I vaguely remember us being raided when I was young, but what my family went through was horrendous.

Although Jim is my brother, he is also an absolute enigma. It's strange to grieve for someone you have never met, but that's the only way I can describe it. I have always heard the stories about him and I've seen the photographs of him. He was a striking-looking young man, very good-looking, and with a wicked sense of humour, but he was kind and good.

Jim was only a youngster when he went into prison. It all began because he was arrested on the day of Bloody Sunday. My mother used to tell us he was walking from Mass when arrested but I reckon he was probably 'dobbing' Mass. In my mother's eyes, Jim was a saint! Well, wherever he was going, there was a British soldier lying on the ground behind a car, crouched down, and Jim tripped over the butt of his gun on the way past and was arrested for assaulting a soldier.

While in custody, he heard the soldiers discussing how people in Derry were going to be taught a lesson later that day, and he was told, 'You're lucky you're not marching or you'd be one of them.' As you can imagine to a young fellow of sixteen, this was unbelievable. It would have got anybody's blood up to hear that innocent people were to be massacred on the streets, and to hear the soldiers making so light of it and saying he could have been one of them.

Jim's own account of what he had seen and heard that day was later found and included in Don Mullan's *Eyewitness Bloody Sunday* book. My mother didn't know this statement existed until the book came out, and when I told her, it broke her heart.

Like so many others after Bloody Sunday, Jim became involved in the IRA. I'm not sure to what level be was involved, as he was only sixteen. Nowadays it sounds ludicrous to put a gun in the hands of a sixteen-year-old boy, but the times were so different back then.

After joining up, he was involved in the blowing up of a filling station in the Waterside – he was the person sent in to warn everyone to get out. As my mother told it, there were two old women in the shop and while he was trying to get them out, he was caught. He was obviously asked to give up the names of his accomplices but he refused. When he was brought to court, he refused to recognise the Diplock court system, so I feel they threw the book at him by giving him four years for his involvement.

Jim was inside from the age of seventeen until just before his twenty-first birthday. He spent time in Magilligan, Crumlin Jail and Long Kesh, and I'm sure he had a lot of thinking time when he was inside. Those were his formative years spent locked away.

I was born in April, five weeks before Jim was released, and I was six weeks old when he was shot dead on 17 May 1976. He was only out of prison a matter of days when he was shot on the bus outside what used to be Fort George. That was five days before his twenty-first birthday. One of the most poignant things I ever heard about Jim was my mother telling me that they had bought in all the food and drink for his welcome home and birthday celebrations, and they had to use it for his wake.

> If the people in power would take the time and listen to the stories of ordinary people like us, they would see this. If we can move on, then they can, too. We can't change the past. What we need to do is learn from the past, move on and work towards peace.

We tried to look into Jim's case in recent years and we went through the Historical Enquiries Team (HET) process, but I didn't feel that it was helpful whatsoever. We do know that before Jim got out of prison, he was told, 'You will be got,' and he was only out a matter of days before he was shot dead. So I believe he was targeted.

He was sitting on a normal Ulsterbus on the Galliagh route to our house when he was shot. Just before this, a girl was shot along the bus route, so the traffic obviously came to a halt on Strand Road to help her, including the bus. That's when Jim and another fella were shot on the bus.

A young soldier was prosecuted for Jim's shooting. He said that he was cracking up and that he thought he saw a gunman on the roof of one of the buildings across the road. The court totally discounted that, though, because the trajectory showed that he could not have seen anything on those rooftops.

I never held any great hope out for finding anything new through the HET report, but even reading things like the Coroner's Report was very interesting for me. I have always soaked up any new bits of information I could glean about our Jim. It is like a jigsaw, a longing to find out what he was really like. People tell me stories about him and I love to hear about him.

It was harrowing for my mother and father. Jim was their first-born. My mother had just had me, too – a new baby – and she was an older mother, so I cannot even begin to wrap my head around how they coped with it all. I do have to say, though, that, as much hurt as Jim's murder caused in the family, there was never, ever any bitterness. We found out that a young soldier really fought to keep him alive, too, which is good to know, but there was no way he could have survived his injuries, he was shot through the neck and the bullet travelled downwards, severing his heart and lungs.

My mother, father and family were so dignified about everything. It tore my mother and the family apart at that time, but we were brought up to get on with things and try to deal with what had happened. I remember once, there was something on TV about a soldier getting hurt, and one of my sisters said something like, 'Good enough for him,' and my mother hit the roof, saying, 'Don't you dare say that. That's some mother's son – that's just like your brother.'

My mother had a great dignity about it all, and she would never have allowed us to revel in someone else's misery. She was such a warm person and saw the humanity in things. She saw another mother's suffering. We owe her so much that we grew up so level-headed and with no bitterness. I would want the same for my children.

I never knew Jim so it's strange for me. I can't describe it, it's like a hollow longing to know him, this brother that I never had. It has always been there. My daddy died when I was eleven, and I remember thinking on my wedding day, 'God, if our Jim had been here, maybe he could have walked me up the aisle and given me away.'

It was tough for the family, and we still feel the repercussions to this day. Sometimes I look at the few photos we have of Jim and I wonder what he would be like now. Would he have a family? What would he do for a living? Would he have had the same wicked sense of humour as me? I think he would have a great wit about him. He must have been clever because he taught himself Irish and was fluent by the time he left prison. He probably matured in there and it was a hard life lesson that he never got to act on.

As far as I know, Jim had spoken to a few cousins after leaving prison and had told them that he didn't think an armed struggle was going to be the way forward. So I like to think he used all that time inside to reflect and see a life beyond the conflict, that he came to a conclusion that there must be another way. If he'd lived, he could have helped make things better here. He could have been one of the great politicians of his time, for all we know. He could have made a difference. Where did all that conflict get us? Where did it get him? Six feet under and no further forward, that's where.

At least today, people are sitting down, agreeing to respect each other, and agreeing to disagree. We're still not there; we have a long, long way to go. But at least we're talking to each other, we're not killing each other, and we are making strides forward. Why didn't we do that years ago and I might still have had a brother?

When I was very young, I remember spending a lot of time over in my older sister Angela's house. Our Angela is dead now, too, but I have so many early memories of dancing to Abba and being spoiled rotten over there. She was about nineteen years older and married, but she treated me as if I was her wee daughter. Looking back now as an adult and a mother, I realise that Angela was helping by taking me off my parents' hands because they were struggling with grief.

I realise now that my daddy was a shell of a man back then. In my mind's eye, I can see him quiet and unshaven, withdrawn almost, and that wasn't him. My daddy would have been very proud of his appearance. He had been in the RAF and had a military way about his looks, always wearing a shirt, tie, and pullover just sitting in the house. In a way, my mother and father were of a very different generation, more like grandparents, because my daddy was born in 1926, and my mum in 1933.

My daddy used to come out with these funny wee phrases, too, like, 'If your hair's neat and your feet's neat, you're all neat.' There was no nonsense with him. However, I can remember when I was very young, he would have sat about the house, dishevelled and down, with a faraway look in his eyes. Obviously, it must have been because of what happened to Jim.

The family went through torture in the weeks and months after Jim died, too. My father's name was also Jim Gallagher, you see, and the British soldiers used to come to our house and stand outside shouting, 'We want Jim Gallagher.' When my daddy went out to them, they'd taunt him and say, 'No, not you. Where's young Jim Gallagher now?' As if our family hadn't been through enough. You couldn't imagine it …

My father died at sixty. I remember him looking dishevelled at times when I was young, which was so unlike him. He was always so clean-shaven, so well dressed. There is a photo of me as a baby sitting on my father's knee, and it always

My big brother was a pencil sketch that hung in our living room

strikes me in that photo that my father looks so old. He was only fifty-one or so then, but he just looks so old and so tired. I often think, what must they have been going through? All that madness to cope with and a new baby, too.

Because I was so young, I was spared the horror of everything really. But even in my earliest memories, I can remember a feeling in the house, like sadness, a paralysis. It's something I wouldn't have understood back then, but I can see now on reflection.

I've always been very open with my children about what happened. They are older now, young adults, and they have always grown up knowing about their uncle Jim and seeing his photographs. I've told them how I feel. The way I feel is that I was robbed of a big brother – that is what the Troubles did to me. I don't blame anyone really, it was a bad time and a bad situation, but there is no point me going through life feeling bitter. I'm not going to lie – I'm angry, I'm sad, I'm hurt, but bitterness is such a useless emotion. There is no point in it. It just eats you up.

I've always told my children about Jim, as much as I knew. I'm still learning new things about him today when I get together with my sisters and they talk about him and all the carry-on they got up to when they were young. They tell stories of how he used to pay them to iron his shirts, or how he would play jokes on them. Finding out bits about him helps make me feel closer to him.

As for my own children, they can't understand my experiences. They find it fascinating to hear about, they study politics and are genuinely interested. But they don't fully grasp how events like this actually touched their own family.

I can see now that there was a strange atmosphere in the house at times when we were growing up, but it got easier over time. Even with a traumatic death like Jim's, it got easier. We got on with it and learned to live with it. My mother never recovered, though.

She had a fantastic, huge pencil sketch of Jim on the wall that someone did and it had pride of place in our house. To me, he *was* this picture on the wall. My big brother was a pencil sketch that hung in our living room. He is just an enigma to me.

I'm not consumed by it, but I do think about him. I remember I was almost afraid to ask my mother and father about him in case it would upset them. If my mother ever heard that hymn, *The Old Rugged Cross*, she would rush to the radio to turn it off because that was the hymn played at Jim's funeral.

My mother died on 12 November 2003 after a stroke. She was in and out of hospital after that, but just went downhill. She had buried her second adult child, our Angela, the year before, so it was just too much for her. She was such a fighter, and we just saw the fight go out of her. She was seventy when she died. The pencil sketch of Jim now hangs in my sister's house.

My mother had a hard enough life as it was, and family really was everything to her. She had grown up in care in Nazareth House in Derry. Her mum did get her out of Nazareth House when she was fifteen, but by then she had tuberculosis and a second family and she basically wanted my mother out of the home to become a skivvy. I remember her telling us once that her mother locked her out in a hen house in the garden and she was starving because she wouldn't feed her. She threw out big floury potatoes to the hens, though, so my mother said she fought the hens for these spuds, she was so hungry.

Once she was back on her feet after the TB, she threw my mother out on the street again. That day my mammy walked all the way to Derry – Derry was all she knew. When she got here, she slept rough for about six weeks. She was sixteen, on her own and homeless. It sounds like something from a film, but she slept under an upturned apple cart. A wee woman called Annie Burke saw her climbing out of this cart a few mornings and cottoned on that she was sleeping rough. Annie took her in to get her washed and something to eat, but when Annie tried to get her shoes off, they'd been on so long they were almost fused to her feet. It must have been agony.

My mother's first job was in the Northern Counties Hotel, and my first job was actually in that building, too, so we came full circle. When my mother met my father, he was her world. My father was from Foster's Terrace down the Lecky Road and he and his brother owned a sweet shop, Sweetheart Confectionary. At the time, potato crisps were just coming out and he charmed her by getting her a packet of crisps! There was a seven-year age difference between them, too, she was nineteen and he was twenty-six. He charmed her and whisked her off her feet – and eight children later – she was still besotted by him. She never dreamt about or looked at another man after he died.

The prevailing message I would like to come from our family's story is that it is possible to deal with the past in a dignified way. It annoys me so much to hear politicians still harking back to the past – the past *is* the past. We have to draw a line under it and move on. If people like my mother and father could remain so calm and dignified, we can, too. They instilled such grace in us and I cannot thank them enough for that. I hope I have done the same with my children. We could very easily have got bitter and hated British soldiers, but what's the point? You're only destroying yourself from the inside out.

If the people in power would take the time and listen to the stories of ordinary people like us, they would see this. If we can move on, then they can, too. We can't change the past. What we need to do is learn from the past, move on and work towards peace.

I would never dream of any other family going through what mine did. I would never dream of one of my children being in the same position as our Jim. Who would ever want to go back to that, being gripped by paralysis as the North was back then? I couldn't care less who is orange or green; if there is a party for peace, that's what I want. I want politicians to stop picking the scab of the past, it's done, and get on with the issues that affect us now. Only when we sit down together, respect each other and listen to each other properly, only then can we make progress.

Eileen Fox

We needed tickets for our own brother's funeral

Since 1969, the Parachute Regiment have killed forty-five innocent civilians, both Catholic and Protestant, in the North – more than the number attributable to any other regiment. On 30 January 1972, paratroopers shot twenty-nine unarmed civil rights demonstrators in Derry – a day now universally known as Bloody Sunday. Fourteen were killed or died from their wounds. A further fifteen people were wounded and two were hit by an army vehicle. Among the dead were seven teenage boys, including Eileen Fox's younger brother, Jackie Duddy – the first teenager to die. Now a mother and grandmother, Eileen reflects on how Jackie's death changed all their lives.

We were a big family: there were fifteen of us in a three-bedroom house with our mammy and daddy. All the girls were in one room, all the boys in another, and for a while, the baby was kept in a drawer, which was made into a carrycot.

No matter what age we were, my daddy would put big old pennies up along our arm on every birthday. The older you got, the more pennies fitted on your arm, and we'd be so excited about this every year, although it was usually the same amount of pennies as your age.

Our holidays were one day to Buncrana. We were so innocent and so easily pleased. On a Friday evening, our oldest sister Maureen would bring home a bag of sweets from Littlewoods and each of us got one butterscotch sweet and were delighted. We had no space and very few clothes, so we had a chest of drawers between us all, and anything we wore had to be washed and hung up to dry straightaway.

Dinnertime was like a military operation. Fair play to my mammy, I remember her trying to call us for dinner, 'Eileen, Susie, Eddie, Jackie, Patrick, Theresa, Gerry …' the names just went on. We needed five loaves and twelve pints of milk every day, and dinner was always made in these huge pots. We took turns at the table at dinnertime, and workers took precedence. Even if we were still eating our dinner, we were told to shift as soon as the workers came in, and, out of respect, we did. Although we didn't have much, we had a dessert every Sunday and a bun on a Saturday. Our baths were on Saturdays, too.

When we went to big school, we had to boil our own socks, and Susie and I used to get Best Dressed awards because we were always so immaculately dressed with our spotless white socks. When we went to Mass, girls had to wear a mantilla, which was like a short triangular black veil. I remember we used to listen to *Top of the Pops* and we would literally get to hear what was Number One, before running down to chapel, grabbing our mantilla on the way out the door. We always had a drawer full of them.

I remember when a visitor called, you were sent down to the shop for biscuits or a slice of ham, because you didn't have things like that in the house ordinarily. We had no such thing as toilet roll in those days, either. We thought a friend of ours was fancy because the newspaper in their bathroom was all cut and hanging up, with cord through it. Ours was just old newspapers.

I was fifteen and studying at the Tech when I first noticed things changing here. My mammy had just died in 1968, which was awful, and my daddy was left with the fifteen of us to look after. This was around the same time as the first civil rights march over the bridge, and things were beginning to happen down the town. My daddy warned us to stay well away, but we paid no heed. We still went down because everybody else was going, too. My daddy would grill us when we came in. 'You weren't down that town, were you?' and we would deny everything, but he knew by our faces that we were lying. He warned us, 'It might be a joke to you now, but it's going to get really bad. It's going to turn to guns.'

He always said that to us, you know, 'It's going to turn to guns.' I suppose he was trying to make us understand the seriousness of the situation, and he was right. He did everything he could to keep us out of trouble. He would tell us all about him being a merchant seaman and that if it hadn't been for England, he wouldn't have had a job. But no matter what he said, we still did our own thing. Although, when the army first came into town, I made a pact with my pals that we'd never go with a soldier, and we never did.

It was always our Susie and I and friends who went to watch the riots – it was great craic to us. We would pull ourselves up onto the windowsills of the old houses on William Street and from there we could watch everything. We would chat about which fellas were out today and who was throwing stones. I fancied Charlie, my husband, back then.

When we ran up the town from riots, neighbours used to put big buckets of vinegar out for people to dip rags into – it helped when our eyes and nose were stinging from the tear gas fired by the RUC in the Bogside, and you'd run from street to street to soak it again quick.

Bishop's Field was right in front of our house on Central Drive, and we enjoyed watching all the people gathering there, too. I think they were getting ready for the Battle of the Bogside, but it was all fun and games to us. It felt exciting – more for the good-looking men than anything else – and we'd be standing around all smiles and giggles.

We were still getting over my mammy dying, and my daddy had no idea about running a house. We all had to help. One day he told me that my family allowance had stopped because I had started further education – so my friend and I went out looking for a job instead.

My first experience of discrimination was that very first job interview. It was with a local bridal and haberdashery shop, and I was fifteen at the time. The man in the shop was lovely and we got on really well, so he gave me the job and everything seemed to be brilliant. Then, on the way out, he said, 'Sorry, miss, I forgot to ask what school you were at before this?' I told him I went to St Mary's in Creggan, and that was it – suddenly he said the job was taken.

It took me hours to realise what had happened. I tortured myself about it all the way home, wondering what I had said or done wrong to ruin it. When I told our boys and my daddy, my daddy didn't spell it out as such, but he did say, 'Do you know what's wrong, love? It's because you're from Creggan – that's all.' He was always very careful not to label things in any way, he would never say Catholic or Protestant, just that we were from Creggan.

Still, nobody was as surprised as I was. I just couldn't believe it. That was the first time I had ever seen or experienced discrimination. I knew it was happening all the time, but this was the first time I had ever seen it with my own eyes, the first time it directly affected me.

Eventually we learned more about Irish history in school, and we formed our own teenage ideas about everything. We realised it was a disgrace the way they were treating Ireland, and we gradually learned that we had to fight for what we wanted – that was something we learned from no age.

I was married in November 1971, just a few months before Bloody Sunday, but we still went back to the family home every Sunday. We loved getting together. On this particular day, it was mostly girls at home – the men were all away to the march – and we were playing cards and listening to *Top of the Pops*, as we always did. I was pregnant with Maureen at the time, or I would have been on the march, too.

Back then, you always stopped and listened to the news, and the radio said that everything was passing by peacefully down the town, so we were relieved to hear it and went on playing cards. Sometimes you could accidentally tune into the army and police radio, too. Their radio broadcasts would come

We needed tickets for our own brother's funeral

through in a crackle, but you could still hear bits and bobs of what they were saying, all boring stuff really.

Then my wee brother Michael came in. He was only twelve then, but he said something about hearing our Jackie had been shot down the town. We all jumped down his throat, shouting, 'God forgive you,' at such a bad joke. Sadly, poor Michael was telling the truth about what he had heard – we just didn't want to believe it.

We tuned the radio in, and we heard the army saying that someone was being carried along Chamberlain Street. Obviously, we didn't know that it was our Jackie they were talking about. Then my husband Charlie arrived. He had left the march early when things began getting out of hand and he saw someone shot. Charlie told us he had heard it on the way up from the town, too.

Then my aunt Dolly and uncle Dusty arrived and told us again, 'We heard your Jackie was shot today.' How they found out so quickly, I don't know. We still didn't believe it, though, and everyone was praying it was a rumour. My daddy was in bed after night shifts, so Dolly went up to tell him, too. We had all been warned not to go near the march, so we knew he'd go mad that Jackie had disobeyed him. We heard him upstairs, shouting, 'I told them not to go! Do they not listen?'

> We tuned the radio in, and we heard the army saying that someone was being carried along Chamberlain Street. Obviously, we didn't know that it was our Jackie they were talking about.

My sister Kay went down to the nearest shop to phone the hospital – to make sure it was true – and the woman at the hospital just said, 'Jackie Duddy? Yes – dead on admission,' and put the phone down. Our Kay went crazy. She had to come in and tell us this, screaming the house down and collapsing. She doesn't remember a thing about any of it, never has.

We were all praying and crying, but at the same time, there was a silence in the house. We just wouldn't believe it, then Kay came back and was half-carried in the door, and we knew it was true. We just lost it. Our poor wee Jackie, he got on with everybody and he was the one who helped everybody, that's what hurt us most. He was never a saint, just a normal bubbly teenager, kind and funny. I think our boys hero-worshipped him a bit because of the boxing, and they were so close, thick as thieves, really. Our wee Michael used to trail around behind Jackie, idolising him. He was seeing a girl from the

Waterside before he died, too. To think we used to panic about him walking her over there, and then he was killed just going down the town.

My daddy and Kay went to the hospital to identify him, Kay holding my daddy up even though she was in pieces herself. Someone, probably out of respect for the dead, had thrown what we would have called 'an IRA coat' – a parka with fur around the hood – around Jackie to cover him up. Just some kind man who had probably lifted him from the street, but my daddy saw this coat and went crazy. He threw the coat off him, and screamed at them, 'Don't you dare try and fix him up!' He thought they were trying to make Jackie look bad. We knew Jackie wasn't involved in anything. We had all been taught about the importance of civil rights and things like that, but we were all cowards otherwise – we wouldn't have dreamt of it.

Afterwards, our house was a maze of people, you couldn't move. There was so many of us and so many people came to pay their respects. Our youngest ones were wandering around, all upset, and everyone was so good to us.

I remember we were sitting crying and my daddy came over and scolded us for being selfish. 'How dare you sit there crying when your mammy only asked for one of you – just one – to keep her company in heaven?' My father might not have said much, but when he spoke, he always said the right thing. That did help us through life, in a way – imagining that she wanted one of us up there with her. I thought that was amazing of my daddy, especially because his heart was broken, too. He was never the same afterwards.

It was ages before we realised how many people were shot and that it wasn't just Jackie. We went around the various wakes and heard the stories about what happened. Until then, we had only heard the army version of events really.

We needed tickets for our own brother's funeral – which was a disgrace – and we were warned not to lose them or we wouldn't get in. The families were sat in the sides of the chapel, too, because the main seats were kept for all the visiting dignitaries. I remember staring at the long row of coffins along the altar ... all these people, killed for nothing.

The Widgery Tribunal was such a slap in the face. We broke our hearts. We put our faith in it – actually believing that they would clear Jackie and everybody else's name, but, of course, that didn't happen. They said he was a nail bomber and that all the others were bombers and gunmen, too. My daddy called them a load of cowboys and told us not to worry, that everyone knew they were innocent. He would say of the soldiers, 'They have a conscience – someday they'll be lying in their death beds and they'll need to tell the truth.' Nobody ever did, though.

There was talk at the time of the parents being offered money to shut them up, but my daddy would never discuss things like that with us. When he died years later, we found all the letters from the Ministry of Defence – they had offered him two thousand pounds for Jackie's death. All the letters were unanswered. He would have seen that as blood money.

In the middle of it all, life went on, but we hated paratroopers. We couldn't relax when we saw them anywhere. I know you can't tar everybody with the same brush, but we had reason not to trust them. They had literally got away with murder the year before in Ballymurphy, too.

We always had Jackie's trophy and showed it to my children and grandchildren growing up, and the hardest thing was having to tell them what happened to him. How do you explain something like that to children? We waited until they were old enough to ask, and eventually we had to, because they'd see the footage of Jackie being carried on TV and saw I got upset.

That was hard. You bring your children up to know right and wrong, and then you tell them something like that – something that sounds so wrong – and you see those innocent faces looking up at you, asking if it's true. I always told them we were still fighting to clear their names, and to always stand up for themselves and to always tell the truth.

I worry for the next generation more than us, sometimes. I was scared they would have hatred against the army – that's why it was so important to look for answers about Jackie and to show them how to fight for their rights. We can't go back to the bombs and the bullets now; we've been there, done it, and we got the vote.

I think the Saville Report was as close as we will ever come to the truth about Jackie. My children and grandchildren were lucky, in a way, because they got to see the results of the Bloody Sunday Inquiry and experience that day and what it did for the people of Derry.

My daddy used to say, 'We're a big family and so if you want to take the happiness, you have to take the sorrows, too.' He was so right. That's probably why we are the way we are today – we're all very positive people and we remain very close to each other to this day.

But this was our wee Jackie, it should never have happened. Sometimes I think of him like Peter Pan – never getting to grow up. I think of him up there, watching us growing old.

Kathleen Brotherton

You could feel that a war was starting

Distance did little to quell the anguish of Irish people abroad when the Troubles erupted back home, and Derry woman Kathleen Brotherton (née McKinney) lost more than most while living across the globe. It was while stationed in Puerto Rico with her American sailor husband Don that Kathleen was told the news that her brother had been murdered back home – on the day that became known as Bloody Sunday. The tragedy was devastating for the family, and became a constant source of worry for Kathleen as she grieved far from home.

I was born in St Columb's Wells and grew up in Westway in Creggan with my two sisters and seven brothers. My parent's names were Mickey and Nancy, and we were a close-knit family. We had to be, because there was one of us born every year! God love my mother, there was no birth control in those days.

I met Don at the Borderland at a dance when I was about eighteen, and when I first met him he asked me to dance to the national anthem! He didn't realise what it was and had got up the nerve to come over to me just as it played, and I said to him, 'Get away – you're showing me up!'

He grew on me, though. He was in the US Navy; I used to see him in Coyle's Café on Carlisle Road, which was a bit of a hangout for Yanks back then. I got to know him, and we got on well. I started going to dances with him, but we had to hide from my father because he didn't allow me to see him – not because he was a sailor but because he was an American. Looking back now, he probably didn't want me to go to America.

Even on my wedding day, my father took me aside and said, 'You don't have to do this, Kathleen, I'll go up and clear out that chapel for you,' and I said, 'No – you will not.' He told me it would be a different story when he was driving me to the airport a year from now – and he was right – it was a whole crying match when that did happen.

Everyone warmed to Don, though. He used to bring over hamburgers from the American Base and so everyone loved to see him coming in our house. We were married in December 1967 and lived in Derry for the first year of our marriage in a flat in Pump Street, with Elaine being born in October 1968.

I remember exactly when I first noticed the trouble starting in Derry. I was in Altnagelvin Hospital having my daughter on 3 October 1968, and the Troubles started on 5 October while I was in hospital. My husband Don couldn't get over to the hospital. When he eventually did, he told me, 'They're tearing the town apart. They're ripping down flags in the Diamond.' It was the Saturday of the first civil rights march, but I hadn't a clue about any of that, I was only twenty-one, and I remember wondering what was going on. Then my mother and father couldn't get over to visit because of the rioting, either.

When Elaine was three months old, Don got word that he was being sent away – to Iceland! We ended up living there for two years and Michael was eventually born there. Before we moved to Iceland, though, we went to Hawaii for a month to see Don's parents, but Hawaii was too far away for me. It was a beautiful place, but I hated it. I just wanted home.

Arriving in Iceland was like landing on the moon. I was twenty-two by then, and the day we arrived, I thought to myself, 'Oh my God, look at this place.' There was not a blade of grass or a green tree anywhere – just a barren, volcanic landscape. It was very depressing. We had to travel for miles just to see a field of grass or anything green – it was always great seeing greenery and life again.

Every three months I would travel home with my daughter from Iceland to Glasgow, then on to Eglinton Airport in Derry. I was so homesick, I needed home. But that's also when I really noticed the atmosphere changing in Derry. Coming home every three months, the changes were obvious. I remember being up in Westway in Creggan when rioting broke out at the police barracks in Rosemount. I remember my mother and other people in Westway putting out wee basins of water and vinegar at the end of each front path for the tear-gassed rioters, with cloths for them to put over their mouths.

There was a terrible fear at that time in Creggan. Suddenly things weren't as light-hearted as just watching riots from afar. It was getting closer. It always worried me to be leaving again and I wished I could bring them all with me. You were always afraid what would happen if you left. You could feel that a war was starting.

We didn't have telephones at the time, so my father and I used to write each other letters all the time, and he would keep me informed of everything that was happening back home. I still have all his letters, too. People back home didn't seem to realise how bad it was. I could see it happening from afar, but they were so used to it, I think they became immune in a way.

We didn't stay in Iceland and were eventually moved to Puerto Rico, and I loved Puerto Rico, it was absolutely beautiful. We were there for three and a half years. We were in Puerto Rico when Bloody Sunday happened. On

30 January 1972, we were getting ready to move to a bigger base on the same island when I got the phone call from my father – he had gone to the American Base in Derry to ring me to tell me what happened.

When he told me, 'Our Willie was killed today,' I think I just presumed Willie had died in a car accident because he was learning to drive. I think I threw the phone up and ran off; I couldn't listen anymore and must have gone into shock. Don must have spoken to my father after I did, and he asked me later, 'Do you know how he was killed?' I told him it was a car accident and he said, 'No, love, he was shot by the British Army,' and I remember thinking, 'Oh, Jesus, Mary and St Joseph …'

> People back home didn't seem to realise how bad it was. I could see it happening from afar, but they were so used to it, I think they become immune in a way.

It was a horrible journey home. I remember telling a woman beside me on the plane why I was coming home – because my brother had been murdered by the British Army. That stands out now. I think she was an American, and she was sympathetic, but I can't remember much. It seemed like the longest flight we ever took. We had to travel Puerto Rico to New York, then to Heathrow then on to Belfast. When we tried to get a taxi at Belfast, nobody would take us to Derry. Everyone refused.

Eventually, one did agree to take us and we got home, and I remember when we came into the city – it was like a ghost town. The place was deserted and all the shops were closed. There were soldiers on every corner with big rifles, and it was like something in Beirut. It was the first time I thought to myself, 'What the hell has happened here?'

When we got to Westway, I dreaded going into our house to face everything. All the others had been buried that morning, but they waited until I got home a day later to bury Willie. It was a shock seeing him in the coffin – it just wasn't like him. He was buried the next morning.

Talking to people, I found out more about what had actually happened and that Willie was taken into someone's house in the Bogside when he was shot. The bullet had ripped his insides out, but I think he lived for about an hour afterwards because Dr McClean and a priest talked to him and gave him the Last Rites. He asked Dr McClean if he was going to die, and although Dr McClean knew he was, he said, 'Sure the ambulance is coming. Don't worry. We'll get you to the hospital …'

Willie was only twenty-seven. He was a very quiet brother, completely different to the rest of us. He was quite the gentleman, always dressed in tie and shirt, and we used to call him the Professor or Specky-Four-Eyes because he wore glasses. But he was a lovely, gentle person, and very private. I would love to have known how Willie would have turned out, what kind of man he became. He was engaged to a girl in the Waterside when he died, too, and it's just terrible that he never got the chance to live or do anything.

It was horrible having to go away again. I had stayed home for a month, and just couldn't settle when I went back. It was a terrible time. I worried more. I worried what else would happen, or if any of our boys would join the IRA because of what happened. None of them did, thankfully. I could understand if they had wanted to, but my father apparently sat them all down and told them that he and my mother couldn't cope if anything else happened – that they weren't to seek revenge – and they didn't. So at least they listened.

We lived in Wales for four years and being Irish was hard. Sometimes you would be afraid to say too much about yourself. I remember visiting one neighbour of ours – she was from Belfast – and as soon as we got to her house she said, 'Well, before we start, I'm a Protestant, what are you?' and I remember I couldn't believe it, but I told her I was a Catholic. She said we would probably get along fine. She came across quite bitter, though, so I never got very friendly with her.

I remember actually being afraid to speak when we were in a bar or restaurant, because all you heard were English accents and everybody seemed to be against the Irish at the time. It was around the time of the bombings in Birmingham, and I suppose I was scared they would think badly of me being Irish. I was paranoid, and I used to think, 'If only they knew what happened to my brother.' I never really talked about that, though. I was afraid what people would think of me. All the Irish seemed to be branded IRA people at that time – especially our families because of what happened – so you did worry what people thought of you. I remember telling my daughter, 'Don't tell anyone about your uncle Willie,' and that was probably because everybody thought they were IRA men at the time, too. It took all these years to clear his name …

I always knew we would come back to Derry. Everywhere we lived, we were trying to get closer to home. We eventually moved back around 1987, and looking back, we had a good life. I was glad to get home when we did, though. I knew the time was right to come back.

Philomena McLaughlin

Sometimes I'm standing ironing and I just cry

From their home in Creggan, the Lynch family had a bird's-eye view of riots near the bottom of their street. Though sheltered from the worst of the early discord, Philomena McLaughlin (née Lynch) was devastated when her older sister was killed while on active duty as an IRA volunteer. Ethel Lynch died on 7 December 1974, five days after being blown up in a premature explosion. She was only twenty-two years old.

I was born in 1958 in Creggan, the youngest of a family of two boys and four girls. My father worked on the quay and was a tough old Derry docker, and my mammy stayed at home and looked after us. We had the greatest family and were always very strong and close.

I was about eleven or twelve when the Troubles started. It began after the first big civil rights march on 5 October, and I remember being in Brooke Park after the swimming baths one Saturday when there was rioting down the town. We began to feel sick in the park; we didn't know what was happening. It was the tear gas burning our eyes. We ran up home crying. My daddy explained to us there was trouble in town, and that the police and army sometimes used gas to disperse the crowds.

We weren't allowed near the town if there was trouble, so when there were riots we'd go down to Brooke Park and sit on the cannons. We had a game of seeing who could sit there the longest before the tear gas burned their eyes. We were probably about twelve then. Mostly we spent our time as children walking out the back roads with a little packed lunch of sandwiches. My mother was from Lancaster in England, so sometimes we would go there for two weeks in the summer. Besides that, we just played in the street.

It was in 1971 that I first actually realised how serious the Troubles were. A family friend of ours, Eamonn Lafferty, was shot and killed in Kildrum Gardens in a gun battle with the British Army as they were trying to come into Creggan. I was thirteen, and that was a huge shock for me. He was my brother Jimmy's friend – and I realised something bad was going on here.

I thought I was going on the march on Bloody Sunday, even though I was only thirteen. My friends and I gathered up at the Creggan shops and the place was buzzing, and all of a sudden, I felt this hand on the back of my neck

– it was our Jimmy. He ordered us home, so we went, and we sat in the street listening to the radio instead.

I remember a neighbour came out and turned the radio station over, saying that people were being shot dead down the town. The adults were all out in the street, talking. Ethel came home first, and then Susie and her husband, and her husband stood against the wall for a minute, and then slid right down it and put his head in his hands and started sobbing.

Our house was pandemonium after that. We knew John Young who had died. He used to collect the coal money every Friday night and it was a fight to answer the door. He was a real looker – a vision with a head of jet-black hair – and when he called, he was always dressed up for his Friday night out. What happened on Bloody Sunday brought it very close to home that things had changed. Lower Creggan, where we lived, had been affected badly. We'd lost young Willie McKinney, John Young and Michael Kelly all from our area, and the older ones in our family had known them.

I remember seeing all the coffins in the chapel, the silence on the day of the funerals – this awful veil over the whole estate – it was a terrible, terrible feeling. A girl in my class had lost her brother, too. None of our house were allowed down the town after that, just in case.

Personally, I think if Bloody Sunday hadn't happened, the Troubles wouldn't have continued for the next twenty or thirty years. People say it became the IRA's best recruitment tool ever – and they're right. People were so angry, there was no other way for them to express how they felt. You went either one way or the other. You could sit on the fence, or you could join the queues signing for the IRA. Who knows, if I had been older, maybe I would have thought that way, too.

God bless my mother. I didn't realise it at the time, but it must have been very difficult for her – as an Englishwoman living in Creggan – seeing what her country was doing to the people she lived among. My mother was at every protest, and when the army came to our door, my daddy always let her answer it because hearing an English accent calmed the soldiers down.

Of course, the Troubles were a horrible thing to live through, and some things will scar you for life, but there were fun times in there sometimes, too. I spent my teenage years in Creggan because we weren't allowed to go anywhere else, but I wouldn't have it any other way. I loved it.

We thought the riots in our street were fabulous. We couldn't go to town, but we didn't need to because the riots were happening right at the bottom of our street and we had a bird's-eye view of everything. There was plenty of talent coming in and out of your house to use the toilet or to get vinegar to protect them from the tear gas. It was great. I remember once, a gun battle started as we were going up Westway to the Sunday night disco. People were shouting, 'Hit the ground,' and I was thinking, 'No, I will not be lying down anywhere with my good clothes on!'

My father was very private about his opinions, while, at that particular time, other people would have been sticking tricolours out the windows on Easter Sunday and things like that. My father always said to us, 'It doesn't matter what you are, don't draw attention to yourself.' That was his view on things. It was just something that we didn't do.

Even as a teenager going down the town, I would wear a wee tricolour pin on my coat. But my daddy would make me take it off, telling us not to go down the town looking for trouble. I had been arrested going through checkpoints on a few occasions for things like refusing to open my coat.

Our house was raided on a regular basis and my brother Jimmy was interned in his twenties. He was arrested in February 1973 and was released on my sixteenth birthday in September 1974. He was interned for a year and eight months. He was always at the front of a riot or coming home with his head split open where he had been hit by a baton. After Jimmy was interned, my mother went to all the protests in town.

Jimmy's internment was felt at home. He was in Long Kesh and had to get a parcel every Tuesday, Thursday or Saturday. There were times we sat down to spuds and nothing else, because we had all agreed that the money was to be put aside for Jimmy's parcels. We were allowed to send him things like toothpaste, soap, shampoo, biscuits and tinned things that didn't go off.

I wrote him letters, and I still remember he was in Cage 8, Hut 65. The letters were sent back to our house with all the cursing scored out, I thought my father was going to kill me, but he and my mother just laughed. I also wrote to my other brother when he did six months for riotous behaviour. I wish I'd kept all the letters now.

On the day Ethel died, a load of us were at home over lunchtime: my mother, Sharon, Ethel, Jimmy and Susie, who was pregnant at the time. I remember Ethel had a bandaged foot and was going to the doctor, and so she walked with me back to school. I remember I told her she was holding me back, dragging that sore foot behind her!

We were sitting in the school library later at St Mary's when we heard the explosion. I remember hearing the explosion, and I looked at my friend Bernie, thinking, 'Oh, God, I wonder if anyone was caught up in that …'

Other girls banged the desks and booed so the teacher told them to calm down.

That was our last lesson on the Monday, and we were walking home when our Susie's husband pulled up in the car. Susie got out and handed me her baby daughter, saying, 'Take her – we're going to the hospital. Ethel burnt herself with a gas cooker in her friend's house and we have to go see how she is.' My mother was in the car, too.

Bernie and I had been planning to go to town, but I took the wain home instead. My daddy was home and didn't even look up when I got in. I asked him, 'Daddy, what's the craic with our Ethel? How come I'm left with the baby?' He just looked at me. I knew something wasn't quite right.

I thought about the explosion, and then I demanded he told me what was going on. Something must have clicked, and I asked, 'She didn't get burned with a cooker, did she?' He told me that she'd been hurt in an explosion, and that my mammy and Susie were away to see how she was.

I think I went on automatic after that, and I still went down the town with Bernie. I remember thinking to myself, 'Jesus, my sister was in an explosion.' I'm sure if something like that happened nowadays, everyone would get out of work and come together, but there wasn't as much communication in those days, just one payphone down the street in Browns' house.

My mammy and Susie came home at 9.00pm that night and told us that Ethel was badly hurt and in theatre. The hospital had sent them home and told them to come back in the morning. These days, you would sit in the hospital all night if you had to – but back then you just didn't do things like that. Besides, the hospital was hiving with police and army. Sharon and I went to see her and she was in intensive care with two Special Branch officers sitting outside the door, and I remember wanting to reach for them. But they allowed us in when we said we were her sisters.

Ethel was sharing a room. There was a big frame over her bed with a sheet over it up to her shoulders, probably to prevent the sheet from touching her stomach where all her injuries were. There were just two small scrapes on the side of her face – that was all – but she looked dead, like she was already laid out for a wake house. All that was missing was the coffin. They had put her in an induced coma. I remember going up to her and blessing myself.

That night I was babysitting for neighbours when the neighbour arrived back and told me to go home. Ethel had taken bad, and my mother was called over to the hospital. The blast had gone up Ethel's nose and down her throat, collapsing her lungs. Although she had severe abdominal injuries, and had lost two fingers on her right hand, she actually died of pneumonia. They had tried to take her off the artificial respirator, but her lungs were too badly damaged and she just couldn't breathe on her own.

She was only twenty-two. That seems so young, but she was actually one of the older volunteers who died – the average age for a volunteer at that time was eighteen. Some were even sixteen or seventeen, so she was old compared to some.

> My father was very proud that we were a strong, republican family, but inside he crumbled.

We were at home when we heard the car pulling up. When I looked out and saw people helping my mother out and down the path to our house, I just knew that Ethel had gone.

How did my daddy react? He just got up and walked out of the room. He wouldn't let us see him cry. He never did … The only time I saw my father express any emotion was in later years, when my mother was showing signs of dementia and we were talking about getting her assessed. We could see the tears in his eyes then. That was the only time. It just wasn't in his make-up to show emotions; he couldn't cope with it.

When we were waiting for Ethel's remains to come home that Saturday teatime, my father took us aside and told us all, 'Before things begin here, I just want you all to be strong, no breaking down, no crying in front of your mother. You all have to remember that your mother had Ethel for nine months longer than the rest of us – and she's going to feel it the worst.'

Ethel was buried on the Monday. I remember very little. I remember being told that she had died, that the house was full of people and that Ethel was in the back room. I also remember that there was always people coming in the back door, and going up to the bathroom to change to do guard of honour. They did a volley of shots for her in Broadway, too.

It was so crowded I couldn't get out of the house when the coffin came down the stairs. I had to go out the back door and through the alleyway, fighting past people, just to get to my family. I don't remember the cemetery, but our Susie says it was snowing. All I really recall about the day she was buried was walking down Broadway later, and saying to my friend, 'Jesus, I can't believe I buried my sister today.'

My mother was a very strong woman. She might have gone to bed at night and cried her eyes out, but she never did it in front of anyone. My father was put on Valium after Ethel died, but my mother took nothing and just got on with things. My father was off work for a few years afterwards, and he had to wean himself off the Valium twenty-five years later. He was very proud that we were a strong, republican family, but inside he crumbled. It took a while to come out, but he suffered so badly.

Do you know, I never asked my mother how she was feeling, either … I never once asked her how she coped when Ethel died. I was probably afraid to ask, for fear of what she'd say. When I look at my own children now, I marvel at how my mother got up the next day after Ethel's funeral and just got on with life.

It was all over the news that there had been a bomb factory in Crawford Square, and people had died in a premature bomb explosion. Ethel was the only person in the house, as far as I'm aware. It was thought that she was the carrier, and they chose a residential area so there was less chance of getting caught. They think that whatever she was sealing into a package must have detonated, and her stomach took all of the injuries.

Two firemen attended Ethel straightaway. I don't know if the blast blew her out into the landing, or she made her way out there, but she was found on the landing and the firemen said her stomach was really bad. There was a lot of blood.

When the doctor and police arrived, Ethel gave the police a false name. It was only when the priest came to see my parents that we found out he had travelled in the ambulance with her and that she had told him her real name. He was saying the Act of Contrition when she whispered into his ear that she was Ethel Lynch from Westway.

We were always being raided after that. Once, we were raided twice in the same day – and I was arrested from the house twice that day, too. People treated us differently sometimes after Ethel died, including some of my friends from primary school, and people whose fathers worked at the docks with my daddy.

We used to be brought into our friends' houses and were allowed to wait while they got ready, but after Ethel died I didn't get in the door. They'd make excuses and tell me my friend would follow me on up to the club, just because they didn't want me in their house. They didn't want that connection to Ethel, and probably thought their house would be raided if one of us were seen in it.

School was a nightmare, an absolute nightmare. One particular teacher picked on me. She would single me out in school and tell the other girls, 'Do you want to end up like her sister? Do you know what happened to her?' Even in the corridor, she'd start on me, until one day I stood up to her, and said, 'This is the last time that you have done this to me.' I walked out of school, and home to tell my daddy, and he calmed me and told me I had nothing to be ashamed of. My form teacher was very good and supportive, though. She sat me down after Ethel died and talked to me, warning me off doing anything foolish.

I was a bit of a militant at school, I suppose. I was headstrong and would have organised walkouts and things like that – even before Ethel died. Maybe it was because our Jimmy was interned, but I just felt really strongly that you should be allowed to show some kind of support – no matter what age you were. I'd tell the teacher there was a protest and eight or so of us would get up and walk out. That was just in our class – I'm sure it happened in other classes, too – I would say that maybe a third of the school would walk out.

Eventually, my form teacher took me aside and told me I couldn't keep behaving like this because it was affecting my education. I told her my family life was affected, too – that my family was being torn apart because my brother was in jail. That loads of other people were in jail, too, and they hadn't done anything. They hadn't even been up in front of a court.

That summer, I was arrested at Beechwood shops when my mother sent me for milk. When they approached me, I started fighting them and was dragged into a Land Rover. I was charged with assaulting three Grenadier Guards and a military policewoman. A Grenadier Guard had to be over six-foot tall and I was only a sixteen-year-old schoolgirl, but I was still charged.

People have suggested over the years that I get counselling but it's not for me. It's not that I've locked it all away – it's always there. There's never a day I wake up and I don't think of her – and of my parents. Sometimes I'm standing ironing and I just cry. I was sixteen when she died, and I don't think it hit me properly until I was married and had children of my own.

I think Ethel became involved because of everything that was going on. She probably decided that, rather than doing nothing, she wanted to try to do something. We genuinely did not know what she was involved in. We thought we were the only ones who suffered. We didn't realise there was just as much suffering and harassment going on around us.

We were always a close family, though. We were there for each other, and that only grew stronger after Ethel died. If anything, it showed us just how important family members are. She left a huge void, but we are extremely proud of her and the sacrifice she made.

Tricia Duddy

I had to share my brother with strangers

Hundreds of republican activists lost their lives during the course of Northern Ireland's Troubles, but behind the statistics are countless siblings and family members who still mourn the loss of loved ones. As the eldest of eleven children, Derry woman Tricia Duddy acknowledges the lasting impact of losing her brother, Charles Maguire, a twenty-year-old IRA volunteer, in a suspected SAS ambush on 28 May 1981.

When I think about my family, I tend to think about November-time. My father always pinned a poppy to the corner of a mirror in our house to remember all his army friends who were killed in the Second World War. He had been in the British Army, too, and so he always went to Remembrance Sunday and would often take us with him. He was shot in the war, but he never talked about it. I regret that we didn't ask him more about those years. My mother's brothers were all in the British Army, too, so we were never a republican family, as such. But we were definitely nationalist.

I remember when I was seventeen and first started seeing my husband Eddie, we attempted to join Eamonn McCann's Young Socialists. You had to be twenty-one to join and needed permission if you were younger, but when the letter came to the house, my father nearly lost his reason and ripped it up and threw it in the fire. 'There's no politics in this house,' was all we ever heard from him.

We weren't a political family and there was nothing overtly political in the house. I vaguely remember hearing what I suppose would be called rebel songs in the house when I was young, my father would sing one or two occasionally, but that was about it.

My brother Charles was the first boy in the house so he was precious. I was eleven when he was born, and my daddy told me I was getting a surprise – I thought I was getting a new schoolbag – and instead I got a baby brother! But we were all so excited because it was a boy after five older girls ... we doted on him when he arrived. When he grew up, his nickname was Pop.

I remember when the Troubles started in 1968 because it was the last time I saw my mother-in-law alive. We'd been to the hospital to see her, but had to get off the bus in town and walk up Carlisle Road through all these riots and water cannon. That was the first big civil rights march on 5 October 1968.

Riots happened regularly after that. It sounds strange to say, but we saw it as entertainment in a way. I don't think we fully realised what was going on. Then one of our relatives was arrested, and after that, things changed for us. We would often be hassled, too.

The police and army tormented our Charles. He was at St Columb's College and everywhere he went, they'd taunt him, telling him, 'When you turn sixteen, you'll be arrested.' They would threaten him with this constantly – that was the kind of life he had.

When he turned sixteen, they did arrest him and kept him in Strand Barracks, but they had to let him out again. This went on and on. When he was in the street, he was always being called after or shouted at. I'm not saying that was his only motivation for joining up, but it didn't help.

It was Ascension Thursday, and a lovely sunny day. Me and my sister-in-law and some of the children had been to Mass, then went shopping and had decided to call into relatives nearby for lunch.

I was sitting at the kitchen table when my sister-in-law Kay came in and stared at me. 'What are you doing here?' she asked. I wondered what she meant, and she said, 'I think there's been an accident – it's something to do with your Pop.' I think she'd already heard because she worked in a shop in the Bogside. They told me to go home, but I didn't want to. Then someone came in and told me my sister was waiting outside for me in the car, but I still refused to go out.

My father-in-law had to come in, and he told me I had to go and listen to what she had to say. I felt it then – I knew it was something bad, and I didn't want to face it. In the car, my sister Isobel told me then that Charles was dead. It was just completely devastating. Everything changed in that instant. He was only twenty, and married with a one-year-old baby daughter.

Driving up home there was just silence, it was an eerie sensation. As we came up through Creggan towards Creggan Heights, there were black flags out on the houses, as often happened back then, and people were standing at their doors. You just felt like everyone was looking at you.

The house was packed. My daddy was sitting there, saying, 'Our son's dead, our son's dead …' he was never the same again. He never got over it.

I remember when we saw Charles; there wasn't a mark on him except for a small plaster on his chin. The back of his head was missing, but you couldn't see that in the coffin, just this one wee plaster. He was buried from his own flat, and there was a continuous line of people going in and out and that was very surreal for me – as if I had to share him with strangers.

To most people, our Charles was called Pop because he was particularly good at the radio quiz, *Pop the Question*. Even his wife called him Pop. I remember during the wake, the army would come past outside the wake, and they had 'Snap, Crackle and NO Pop' written on their helmets, like the cereal. That was just unbelievable.

The wake was very difficult because we couldn't be on our own with him. He had a guard of honour who stayed there throughout, so there was no privacy. I understand how important this tradition is, and that it's a mark of respect, but I think it's very hard for the family who get no time alone with them – no time to absorb it. I didn't like it. He was my brother and I didn't want to have to share him with all those people, which I know was probably selfish of me.

My mammy and daddy thought differently, though. I think they got comfort from the fact that so many people came to show their respects and that there was so many people around. It helped them to know that so many people cared.

It was a double funeral for Charles and George McBrearty, the friend who was killed alongside him, and I remember the crowds walking up the road. We were carried away in this very public event. But in our own private grief, it felt unreal, like the whole thing was taken out of our hands – we felt like bystanders at his funeral. It was as though I was watching a film. It was only afterwards, when we were finally left alone at the graveside, did we have the time and space to think at all.

> I was always petrified that our boys would lose their tempers, and the army would do to them what they did to Charles. Thankfully, neither of my other brothers went down that road.

My father was a broken man afterwards. My mammy was, and still is, the backbone of the family. She's eighty-five now and still lives in Creggan and she is an incredibly strong woman. She helped everybody through that time and kept everybody together.

Because of what happened to Charles, you never got over that fear of soldiers or police. When you saw them, you would panic a bit and your heart would miss a beat – worrying what could happen. They would come in to raid or hassle you, just because of who you were. I remember when the police were in our house once, they told me I was very well placed – as a schoolteacher – to hear certain information. They said that I could help fill in pieces of jigsaws for them if I told them what I saw or heard. I nearly died, and refused, of course.

My brothers were always being stopped and intimidated. One of my brothers lived in England and he used to miss so many flights there and back because they would stop him and hold him at the airport, just because they could. I was always petrified that our boys would lose their tempers, and the army would do to them what they did to Charles. Thankfully, neither of my other brothers went down that road.

Charles was a lovely fella, very good and kind. He was very funny and very clever, but he could be grumpy, too, and didn't suffer fools gladly. At the time he died, he was very close to my three-year-old son and would have taken him into town to see the Christmas lights at Austins Department Store and things like that. If he had lived, he would have been a brilliant father.

Charles' baby daughter was the biggest blessing to everyone. She was meant to be here – she kept everybody together after he died and gave us a focus. My daddy just adored her. She was special – because she was Charles' – and as a grown-up, she is like her father in so many ways.

My children have always known of Charles and my grandchildren recognise his photograph now, too. It was important that they knew who he was. Every Easter Sunday we go to the memorial at the City Cemetery and our children and their children come, too. I think it's important that things like this continue down the family – that the younger generations know and remember, too.

I tried my best not to pass any fear of soldiers on to my own children. We've always tried to be honest and tell them what happened, but in such a way that they wouldn't feel the same fears and dreads that we did. I still feel it today, though. I met a woman in a waiting room recently, and we struck up a conversation. It was all going well until she told me that her son had been accepted into the SAS. I was horrified. 'They're the elite of the elite, you know,' she said. I fought the urge to say, 'Oh, yes, and they're murderers, too.' But I said nothing to her – who would? Instead, I made my excuses for the loo, and I just sat somewhere else when I got back.

I think the women in Derry have always been very strong – they had to be. My mammy is an amazing woman; our house would just fold without her. We worry every time she gets sick nowadays, because she's getting older, but she's still here and happy, and she's the strongest woman I ever met. There were many times I worried that my mammy and daddy wouldn't survive the grief, but my daddy lived another sixteen years after Charles died. He never stopped thinking about him, and when he was dying he mistook another brother of ours for Charles, he must have missed him so much.

When Charles died, I understood just how awful grieving was. I never realised how much it could hurt. It never goes away. You get used to it, but even today when I talk about him it still feels as fresh and raw as it ever was. I do still think about him at family occasions and times like that. I think about him missing it all. Our family photographs since have never been the same. We're all there – but he's not.

We've always been a very strong, close family anyway, but we became stronger because one of us had gone. We clung to each other for support and help – we still do. But he was always missed.

Family is everything, and life has taught me that you need to keep your family close to you. Appreciate the people around you, and don't let trivial things get in the way, because it can all change in an instant. You can lose people so easily. We'll never have Charles back again.

Women's Reflections

I don't know what the future holds for Northern Ireland because the politicians just can't agree. They can't even talk but they end up fighting. Our young people need more opportunities. I'm not sure if there even is peace nowadays.

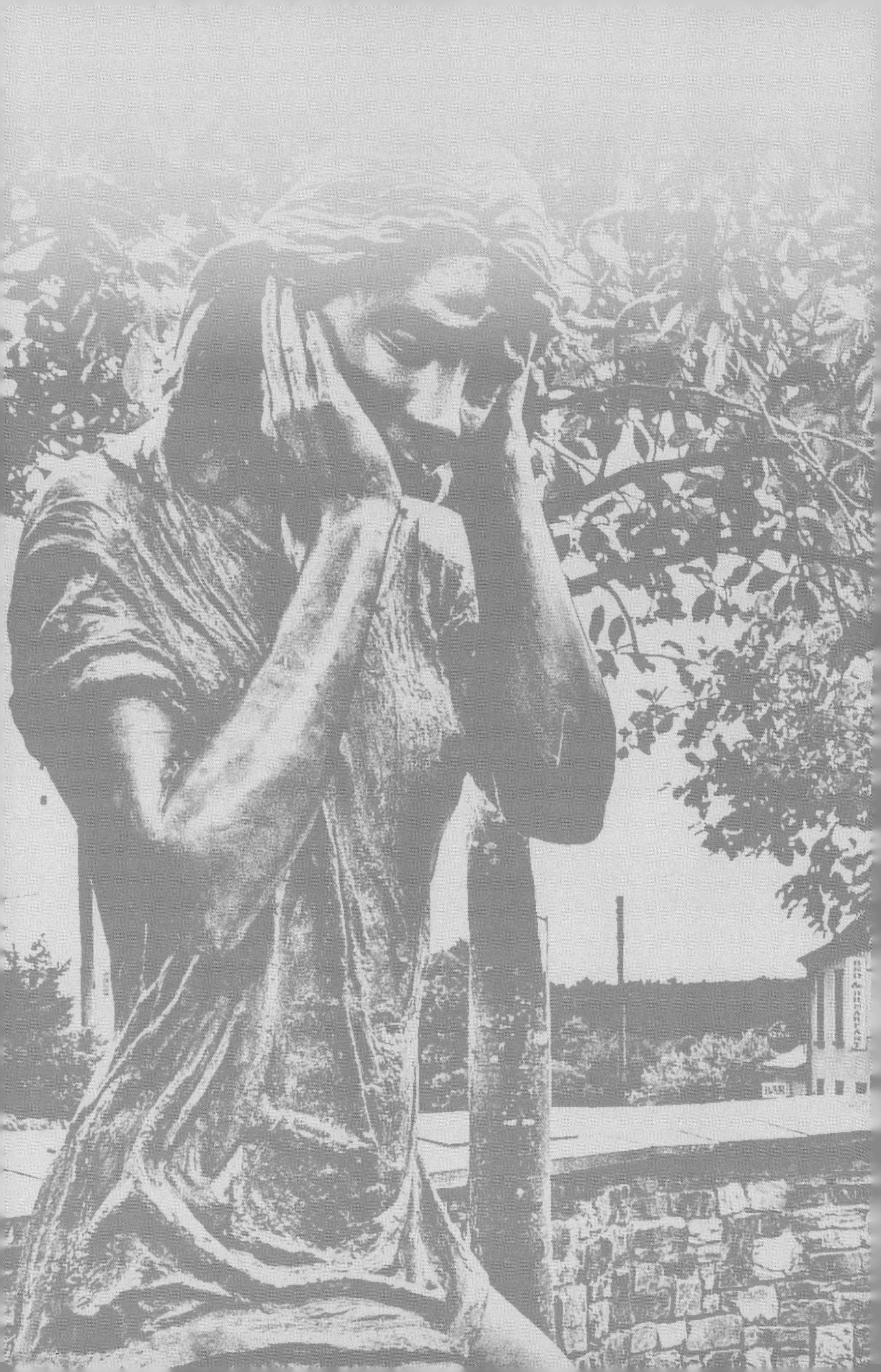
BAR

Ruby McNaught

Those were the days, my friend

After rearing her family, Derry woman Ruby McNaught went back to school and rediscovered her own career in teaching. During her working life, she worked as a co-ordinator for NATO, organising educational visits between the University of Ulster and Brussels. Back in the 1950s, Ruby's family were among the first to move into the new housing estate of Creggan – a haven for the city's growing Catholic community who struggled to find adequate housing. Here, she shares fond memories of growing up in the Creggan of a bygone era – long before the Troubles took hold.

My mother and father were married on 15 January 1939. My mother came from a well-known family, the McCaffertys of the Lecky Road, and my father's family, the McLaughlins, were from the Lone Moor Road. Both were large families, with eight or nine children in each.

My father was a pipe fitter by trade, but he always worked away because there was no employment in Derry. My parents' lives consisted of long separations while he was working in England, and I suppose in that way they were very much the same as so many other couples at the time – the husbands away working while women were left behind to rear the children.

In the early 1940s, when they were first married, my parents moved into the Lecky Road with my mother's mother, a two-bed terrace house with nine other adults. By 1949, my mother had three girls and one boy, and so, obviously, my father's trips back from England were very useful. They badly needed a home of their own, and so, when it was decided to build houses in Creggan, my mother immediately put her name down and prayed incessant rosaries that she would be granted a home of her own.

When the letter arrived to say that she got a house in Creggan Broadway, she was ecstatic. It was like winning the pools. When she rang my father from the call box, he was delighted, too, and he made the decision that he would finish up in England, and try his hand at painting and decorating back home in Derry.

The day we got the keys, we all traipsed up Bligh's Lane to our new house in Creggan. There were no taxis in those days, because you just couldn't afford them. I remember the day well – we sang and laughed the whole way up.

Those were the days, my friend

When the front door was opened, we were dumbstruck by the size of the rooms and the luxury of the kitchen and the bathroom – the likes of which we'd never seen before – and a separate toilet!

The kitchen had a large sink, so high up that we couldn't see into it. My mother squealed when she saw it, 'Oh, dear! Look at the jawbox!' That's what they called those Belfast sinks in those days. The living room was enormous with a small fireplace, which, in hindsight, never really heated the large room. We moved in that very day with bits and pieces of furniture given to us by various relatives.

> We were dumbstruck by the size of the rooms and the luxury of the kitchen and the bathroom – the likes of which we'd never seen before – and a separate toilet!

Later that day, a big Cavendish's van arrived with a two-seater sofa, two chairs in leatherette and two beds, all bought on tick – credit, that is. We all ran about excitedly as the man brought in our new furniture. We eventually went to bed after playing in our beautiful garden until late that night. We could hardly sleep with the excitement of our own bedroom. It was heaven.

When I think back to that small living-room suite, it hardly filled the room, and the lino was very cold on the feet, no carpet for us. There was no central heating, either, so the house was always cold, but it was filled with love and happiness.

My father used to get up in the morning, light the oven and leave the oven door open to heat the kitchen while we had our tea and toast. We had very little, but all the families in the Circle, as we called it, were the same. No competition with their houses, no cars, everybody was in the same boat and struggling to survive. But we had a home, and that was the most important thing.

We had a lovely green area in front of our houses, where we played games and had picnics. Our neighbours were fantastic, a mixture of Catholics and Protestants, all poor but happy. We kids were all great friends, we played with each other's toys, and we went for picnics to Holywell Hill with jam sandwiches and a bottle of water. We collected blackberries and often came home with sore bellies, tired but happy. In the school holidays, my neighbours organised games in the green. My mother baked, as other mothers did, so we had fairy cakes and jam sponges, too.

The women never went out socially in those days because there was never enough money and they didn't drink. But they enjoyed a cigarette, and they went to each other's houses and gossiped. On a Friday night, my mother, and her friends Rita and Ruby, would all walk out over the border to the Black Hut in Killea to smuggle back butter and cigarettes. It was like a social outing to them, and they walked there in summer and winter. I often heard them talking about the craic they had, and how they would dodge the customs men patrolling the border!

We had five happy years in Creggan, before tragedy struck and my father died aged thirty-nine, in the City and County Hospital. Mum was only thirty-six and left with six kids to rear, aged between fourteen and the baby of eleven months. All the friends in the Circle rallied around my mother and offers of help came from all parts of Creggan.

The Widow's Pension was very small and there were no benefits in those days. A part-time job in the factory wasn't enough to survive on, so my mother decided to look for a house swap to be nearer her own mother – that way, our granny could watch us, and she could work full-time. Despite us moving away from the area, Rita and Ruby remained my mother's dearest friends until she died.

I have great memories of Creggan. It was a proud place and a great place. A place of fantastic people who shared what they had with each other. The men unemployed, women working in the factory, and all with the same goal – to rear their families with love and respect.

I had my first kiss at the bottom of Broadway, my first pair of nylons there, too. Those were the days, my friend. I'm sorry they ended.

Nan Duncan

I picked my children's friends

Being a mother and role model can often be the most challenging job of all, but like most women, Anna 'Nan' Duncan, saw it as a wonderful gift. Born in the rural townland of Newtowncunningham, Nan and her siblings were delighted to make the move to the nearby city of Derry/Londonderry in the 1950s. Now a grandmother, she reflects on rearing children through volatile times, and the importance of being their 'mother, father and friend'.

My father was away most of the time as a chief petty officer in the navy, so in 1953 the whole family moved in from the country to Northland Drive in the city. We already went to the Model School anyway, and we travelled there and back every day by bus with our couple of lumps of jam scone.

When I left school, I worked in Littlewoods in Waterloo Place until my second child was born and I loved it there. I worked at the wool counter, and every day I walked down to the town in my high heels, walking back up to Northland Drive again at dinner time, and then again at home time.

When I was nineteen, I met my husband-to-be, Ernie. His real name was actually Armour, but he was called nothing but Ernie his whole life. We met when I piped for a band in Newtowncunningham and Ernie came in for the day when we needed an extra piper. I noticed him the minute he walked in the door. We got engaged that October and married in April, and we had sixteen years and seven children together.

When we got married, we lived in one room in a townhouse in Florence Terrace, opposite Magee University. It was all I needed, and I would be quite happy to be back there now in that one room again. I had two children, and was ready to have my third by the time I eventually started fighting for my own house.

When Andrew was a baby, I was walking to my mammy's, past Crawford Square, when a car came around the corner. The people in the car looked at me and I looked at them, and then they drove on and came around again. When I got to my mother's house, I heard that local businessman Joseph Glover had just been shot dead at his office in Crawford Square.

I had seen that car. It had an English registration, and I tried to memorise the number plate as it passed. I remembered most of it, but not all. This was stuck in my head for a long time. When I went to bed at night, I still couldn't sleep. I was still trying to remember that bloody number. It was there subconsciously, but I couldn't get it.

We felt the trouble closer to home, too. I think it was around December 1987 when we had a few bombs where we lived in Tullyally. They were meant for security forces, two of them went off and one was found before it detonated. When the first bomb went off, people naturally ran out their front doors to see what happened. The windows had come in, and there was glass all over our house and the children's bedrooms. I automatically thought about my daughter, who lived nearby – so I took to my heels and ran up there. A friend of mine saw me go out and pulled me back. If he hadn't pulled me back inside I'd have been blown to bits because then the second bomb went off up the street at my old house.

> If I saw them playing with certain people, I'd bring them in and they'd stay in ... I was glad I did, too, because the same people I warned them off when they were young did end up in the UDA or other organisations.

The man who lived in my old house had come out to look around after the first explosion and was caught in the second bomb – and he was killed. He was the only Catholic in the street. They'd planted the bombs in the wrong street, apparently. They were meant for security forces in Milltown Crescent but they were accidentally put in similarly numbered houses in Milltown View.

None of my children were hurt, thankfully, but my son Andrew was affected. He took some kind of funny turn and had to go to hospital. I've often thought about it since, wondering if that early shock was the beginning of his cardiomyopathy, even though it wasn't diagnosed until his twenties.

My steel window frames were all warped because of the bombs and needed replaced, but compensation didn't pay for all of it, so we ended up in debt, too. Eventually, I got my three-bedroom house in Milltown View, just a street away. We used the pram to move all our things, pushing it back and forth up the footpath to our new house.

We went through a few scratches really. Once, we were driving in Foyle Road with all the wains piled into the back seat of the car – there were no seatbelts then – when IRA vans at the bottom of Bishop Street stopped our car. It was very scary, because they were all wearing masks and had guns. One of them came over and looked in, but then told us to go on. I was so scared, though.

I was determined to keep my children out of trouble. I had two boys and I picked their friends. That was important to me because of the times we lived in. I would not allow them near anyone I had any inkling about, and I had to be really strict about who they could hang around with.

I warned them that, if I saw them playing with certain people, I'd bring them in and they'd stay in. I was glad I did, too, because the same people I warned them off when they were young *did* end up in the UDA or other organisations. I suppose it's the same as the Roman Catholic side – parents worrying about their children joining the IRA. Well, I was terrified that my children would be swayed towards the UDA, and I am glad I was so strict with them. I had no time at all for paramilitaries, no matter who they were. I still don't.

My husband Ernie worked for the Water Board and once when he was up in the Top of the Hill area, the IRA held him up at gunpoint and burned his van out. He was badly shocked by this, but he was lucky he wasn't shot because they all had guns. Ernie died a year later, aged just forty, and I sometimes think that the shock of that night might have triggered off his cardiomyopathy. A few weeks before he died, his doctor told him there was nothing wrong with him and gave him tablets for his nerves.

We tried to make a happy home without him. I tried to be mother, father and friend to my children over the years, and I think that worked.

Hilda Campbell

Mayhem, memory and the Bay City Rollers

Hilda Campbell was born and raised in the heart of Creggan, and despite it being a major flashpoint during the conflict, she has always loved the area. In fact, today she still lives in the same street – just across the road from the family home where she was born. Here, Hilda reflects on growing up in a time of great change.

I never moved very far. Creggan was a brilliant place and we loved it here. I had seven brothers and six sisters, one brother was stillborn and another died aged three and a half. Today I have three brothers and five sisters.

We weren't a very political family, but my da was very strict. We had to be in very early when we were young, and I can still see us up in our beds, looking out the windows at all our friends still out playing in the street.

I remember when the British Army first came in 1969 and we started seeing them around. You heard the sound of the Saracens before they came. At the start, when they were at the bottom of our street in Cromore Gardens, the local children were playing with them and talking to them. They'd give you sweeties or chocolate, and the local women would make them tea and cakes. But that soon changed.

I remember Bloody Sunday, but I wasn't there. I remember all sorts of things, but I wasn't there. I only knew about things because I saw the photos and the papers. Because my da was so strict, we were sheltered in the house – that's just the way it was. They wanted us to be safe.

When I was sixteen, I remember being out in the street and having to dive, flat to the ground, so we wouldn't get shot with bullets whizzing over our heads. It was like a gun battle, you could feel the bullets flying past you. That happened loads of times and it was so scary. Life was crazy in general back then. I remember they used to shoot CS gas outside our house, and they would deliberately shoot it at dogs, too, so they would bark and bark.

Another time, we were stopped and the army wanted me to open my coat. They threatened to arrest me because I wouldn't let them search me. I refused of course, and then, when I eventually gave in and tried to open my coat, the zip stuck! That's just the kind of thing that happened in those days, it was normal really. It seems madness when you think back.

Mayhem, memory and the Bay City Rollers

Before the Troubles, everything was great. I loved that time when I was growing up. I was born in the 1960s and I really enjoyed my life. I met Danny and it was puppy love. Then I met him a couple of years later and we got together. I loved life, I loved the Bay City Rollers, and I had the tartan trousers, the boots, the lot. I loved them. I remember when Danny and I were teenagers, getting our black oxford shoes tipped and heeled, and us clicking up and down the street in them, wearing our Crombies. I loved those years.

> I remember when Danny and I were teenagers, getting our black oxford shoes tipped and heeled, and us clicking up and down the street in them, wearing our Crombies. I loved those years.

We panicked when I found out I was pregnant and wondered what we were going to do because we weren't married. We told Danny's mother, and she just kept saying, 'My Danny? *My* Danny?' She couldn't believe this – maybe she thought he was going to be a priest or something …

Then I had to tell my own mother, so I told my sister and she told her for me. Then, when I was going out to work, my mother said to me, 'So you're pregnant? How am I going to tell your father?' Every day when I came in from work after that, I'd ask her, 'Did you tell my daddy yet?' but she hadn't. When we did eventually tell my daddy about the baby, he just said, 'I wish that was all the bother I had.' Compared to some, he took it well.

My mum wouldn't let us get married until we had the baby and saw how everything worked out, so we waited and got married when the baby was six months old. We got married at nine o'clock in the morning and had a big breakfast back at our house, just our families and us. My daddy took us to the PO Club that night and we had a wee shindig there, then it was back to Danny's sister's where we and the baby were staying. Danny had sausage and chips and I had fish and chips – sitting in bed! That was the extent of our honeymoon. I was married about three months when I fell pregnant again.

Married life was good, but you do have to work at it. When I look at young ones these days, they just don't work at it anymore, and marriage takes work. Divorce is an easy option. We worked at it, and we're still here. I have six children, five girls and one boy. My boy was born on Christmas Day.

When I was about three months pregnant with my first daughter, something kicked off while I was at Creggan shops and I was hit by a bit of shrapnel from a blast bomb. It cut my chest, not badly, but they couldn't X-ray me for shrapnel because I was pregnant. It felt like a huge, powerful force, and even though I wasn't badly hurt, many other people were.

Two of my children were playing in the street once, too, when men accidentally set a bomb off in their car. I ran like hell down there, and all the children were hysterical. It was terrible that something like that happened while they were playing in their own street. Luckily, the explosion went upwards and not outwards, or some of the children could have been killed.

I am very protective with my own children. I'm a bit of a worrier, as all mothers are, I suppose. It's just instinct. Especially with my youngest, she has to ring me all the time to let me know where she is and where she's going. I worry all the time.

I'm not a political person, but at the end of the day, I do agree with the peace process. We have to keep looking for peace – for our children and for others growing up now. For our children, there is no more rioting and no more bombs, they're not going through what we did. I know there are still incidents here and there, but we need to move on.

Communities do still have problems today, but I think the problems are different now. When we were growing up, we didn't have all the added dangers of drugs that exist nowadays. In a way, they're even worse than the bombs. But I'm happy that my children grew up in a safer time than we did. They have a better chance.

Jane McMorris

It's good that women are beginning to talk now

Raising a family in the heart of one of Derry/Londonderry's interface areas, Jane McMorris faced the perils of conflict every day. From their home in Irish Street, the family faced a fusillade of missiles and bullets aimed at barricades outside. Now in her seventies, Jane reflects on her life experiences.

I was reared in Cullion, near Donemana, with my two sisters and two brothers. We went to a very small school there with just two classrooms in it. There were no dinners at school then, so we used to 'scobie' the turnips on our way home because we were starving, or get apples from one of the orchards.

We were very isolated in the country. We had no electric, just Tilley lamps, and we kept our milk in a little stream across the street. Our toilet was outside, too. Every day we went to a well to get our drinking water, and the trick was to make sure we didn't spill any of the water on the way.

We didn't have much at Christmas, an apple or orange and maybe a wee doll. I remember when Maltesers came out – we thought they were great! But we were always happy. We made our own fun and made the most of everything. My mum used to play rounders with us, using a spud wrapped in a pair of her tights!

My sister got me a job in Welch's factory in Derry, and so I used to travel in by bus. I also worked in Selfridge's Fish and Chip Shop, which is where I met my husband, Richard Edward, from Glendermott Road, and he asked me to a dance at the Memorial Hall. He would travel out to mine on the bus, and I would come into town on the bus, so it wasn't an every-night romance. We were married after three years when I was twenty-one. Everybody knew him as Sonny, but I called him Herbie. I remember the first time I saw a television when I visited Herbie's house – and I thought it was just fantastic!

We lived in Rose Court in Gobnascale when we got married, and I remember seeing the army first coming in, the boys swarming down the street towards Spencer Road. We were in Gobnascale when Bloody Sunday was happening and could hear all the shooting over the town. Our neighbours took us to their upstairs flat, in case our flat downstairs came under attack.

When Niree was born, we moved to Campion Court. Around that time, the IRA threatened my husband on his way home from seeing his mother, so then we knew we had to get out of Gobnascale.

There was a Catholic family living in our present house. They were getting hassle for being Catholic here, we were getting hassle for being Protestant there, and so we asked the Housing Executive could we swap with each other. Within two weeks, we had swapped houses, and it was just easier to live here. It was an easier, safer community for our family at that time.

I have seven children, four boys and three girls. We didn't have much, but we made the most of everything we had. I remember having to give the children crisp sandwiches for their dinner at times, because we just didn't have very much money.

We had no problem with Catholics and Protestants. We have both in our family, so it was never an issue. We just wanted an easy life. But Catholics who sometimes came into the area were targeted, so we had to try to get them out safe. People came from the Top of the Hill to throw stones, then there'd be bombs up the street, too, and the whole street was evacuated. We had to get up and get the wains out in the middle of the night to go and stay with my husband's mother.

I remember once, when I was pregnant with our Stephen, I was stoned by people from Gobnascale while walking down Fountain Hill to the Health Centre. I held my stomach and ran like the dickens! That was scary.

The biggest thing to happen around here was when the barricades went up across the street. At the top of Bann Drive and Mourne Drive, a big lorry and barricade permanently blocked the road, and they would shoot down towards our street from Gobnascale. You couldn't use the front of the house because of it.

We got our windows broken so many times. Sometimes the children were in the room when it happened and they'd have to lie down on the floor, or go into the back room and stay there. They were often scared stiff and in hysterics. It was usually bricks and stones. One night the army was involved in firing rubber bullets, too, and we were caught in the crossfire. The window glass hit our Venetian blinds before it reached the room. It was terrifying. Thankfully, none of my children were injured.

I wouldn't let them out anywhere when there was trouble, and I made them stay in the back room if anything was going on. It was very scary as a mother, knowing that this could happen and your children could be hurt.

Petrol bombs were the scariest. One of our neighbours got a petrol bomb thrown through their window, and another neighbour had their car burnt out, too. Basically, anybody who lived along our front row was in danger.

Once, we were coming home from a night out and we literally couldn't get across the street. We had to get down on our hands and knees and crawl across the road to get home – and you could hear bullets whizzing the whole time. I remember knocking on the door when I got there, shouting, 'Will you open the door and let us in!'

> We had no prejudices – it was other people's prejudices that caused all the problems.

I remember when news came through of hunger strikers dying; people would come out onto the streets with their bin lids and whistles and stand right across from us on the interface. When things like that happened, we had to go out the back door and run to my husband's mother's house. You just didn't know what to expect. My wains were only young so we got out of there, just in case.

Of course, there were Protestants fighting back at the top of the street, too. They were mostly young men really. I never looked out – you couldn't look out anyway, in case you were seen. If anything was happening, the neighbours would help spread the word, and it was a close community in that way because everyone looked after everyone else.

Even when we moved away from there, we were still friendly with some of our old neighbours in Gobnascale. We had no prejudices – it was other people's prejudices that caused all the problems. For example, they accused my husband of bringing information from Gobnascale to Irish Street when he was checking on his mother.

My husband had heart trouble, so he wasn't well. He had valves put in his heart, but it didn't work. He wasn't allowed near metal detectors at any of the checkpoints in town because of his heart. It would have stopped the ticking. You could actually hear him ticking – like a time bomb.

In 1982, he died of a massive coronary in the bed beside me. He was only forty-three and I was left with seven children. The night he died, I ran out in my nightdress and bare feet to call for help from the police who were always stationed outside. An ambulance came and the crew worked on him, but it was too late.

That was a terrible time. My daughter Niree was in America, and didn't get home until two weeks after her father died, because she was too young to be allowed to travel home on her own. One of my sons was away with Holiday Projects West, too, and had just come home that morning.

After my husband died, I ended up in Gransha Hospital for fourteen weeks with a nervous breakdown. I was probably in my late thirties then, and Doris, my eldest girl, was about eighteen and had to look after the other children while I was away. A social worker kept check on them, too.

I felt stronger when I got out. With God's help, I got through it, although my children would probably say I spent too much time up in Altnagelvin cemetery. I don't go up there as much now ... But after my husband died, I never went out anymore and I lost all my confidence. I'm happy enough in the house.

I try to get out more these days, and it is nice meeting new people, but I still find it hard to make conversation with new people. It's good that women are beginning to talk now – we have a lot to say.

Anna Gallagher

We felt like hostages every day

Targeted for being a republican family, Anna Gallagher's family were frequently harassed by the British Army in their Creggan home during the past few decades. Born the second youngest in a family of four, Anna feels that the stress of this constant intimidation affected not just their childhood, but their education, too.

We were raided every morning for years. I was only six or seven at the time, but I still remember it. We felt like hostages every day, with Brits in and out of our house constantly, going through everything we owned. We were targeted because we were a republican family. We always had people staying with us, too, and it was a bit of a halfway house in that way. Quite often, we would have woken up in the mornings and stepped over people in sleeping bags in the living room.

The Brits would bust in the front door and we always had to replace it, so my daddy eventually copped on, and made sure that we were all up and ready when the Brits landed – and opened the door to let them in. That's probably where my clean-freak habit comes from – we were made to get up early, make the beds, make sure everything was spotlessly clean, and, 'Give those British bastards nothing to say about us.' My own girls have been cleaning since they were able to walk, too, so that's obviously where it stemmed from. I've passed on my OCD to them, too.

The army being in your house is intimidation enough – a big squad of men taking over and going through everything you own. The soldiers would be really rude to us, but I suppose we would be equally rude to them, too. They were known for planting guns and stuff, and even at that age, we were always told to follow them and watch to make sure they weren't planting anything. They would search drawers, pull apart beds and search every single corner. I was just a wee child, wandering about in the middle of all this, and I remember I just felt harassed and wondered why we couldn't live a normal life.

They even came in the morning of a family wedding and harassed the whole house. They messed the bride's dress out of pure badness, and the soldiers wouldn't let my mammy get out of the bath, either.

I hated the army being here. Hated it. When Saracens arrived in the street, people would riot and I'd be out along with them, joining in, and that made me feel better. It wasn't just our house they raided, and there were more and more riots, Saracens, jeeps and barricades. It was everywhere.

Around the time of the Long Kesh hunger strikes in 1981, my father witnessed what happened to Gary English and Jim Brown at a riot and had to go through a whole court case afterwards. They were hit by the same Saracen, which then reversed over Gary English, killing him. Jim Brown was killed at my father's feet. The Saracen sent him flying and he literally landed at my father's feet, and my father took that very badly. He had to testify, and the trial really took its toll on him and his health deteriorated.

> They would search drawers, pull apart beds and search every single corner. I was just a wee child, wandering about in the middle of all this, and I remember I just felt harassed and wondered why we couldn't live a normal life.

I remember being in a bar with my mammy and daddy, when I was about twelve, and young men who'd been shot by rubber bullets were brought in. There was blood running out of them everywhere, and everyone pitched in to take care of these teenagers. I was only young, but I remember.

The situation interfered with school. I went to St John's Primary School, and the army were there on so many mornings before I went to school that I went to school all annoyed. I think it was probably the same for everyone caught up in the Troubles at that time – it really affected people's education. I wanted more education. I wanted to learn and better myself, but I could never settle down. I found it difficult to concentrate at school, there was always so much going on in my head. It was too hard to focus.

I cared more about education in later years, but even to this day, I can't concentrate properly. I can't seem to keep anything in. I only ever got an O-Level in Irish, and that's probably because that's the subject I was interested in at school.

When I got older, I wanted to join the IRA and fight the war. I was probably about eighteen then, and I seriously considered it for a while, but I never did. Now that I'm older, I'm glad I didn't join up because I probably would have ended up in prison or somewhere.

Until now, I've always blanked this stuff out and pretended it's not there. It's not just what happened at home, it's what happened every time you went up the town shopping, in William Street, Chamberlain Street, the Bogside, riots – always riots, every day of the week. What did I feel? I felt hatred … It's still there. I just hate the British forces, the British, the RUC, the PSNI. It's in my memory all the time, it'll never go away. I have two daughters, and I worry that if the Troubles were still going, they would be involved. I'm glad they're not, obviously.

    I know there is a peace process, and I do hope it works, but as long as Ireland is occupied, there will always be trouble.

Anonymous

Everything seemed to change overnight

Movement of people and families has always accompanied conflict. In terms of the Troubles here, many families have stories of such displacement, and, in spite of the Good Friday Agreement, we still have conflict-related displacement today. Like most children, 'Ellen' (not her real name) loved the neighbourhood she grew up in and the myriad memories created there. However, the security of this childhood home came to an abrupt end in the 1970s, when her family were forced to flee their home on Derry/Londonderry's east bank.

I can still see my father crying when we were told to leave Top of the Hill … He was heartbroken. He loved that house, and he got on so well with all our neighbours.

I was probably eleven and in my last year of primary school when we lived there. We had plenty of Catholic friends and everyone got along. I even remember my mammy taking the Catholics down to the 12 August celebrations with us and giving them a flag, and us sitting on the pavement together, enjoying a big day out. Everything seemed to change overnight.

Suddenly, we didn't feel safe living in our own house. When I was out playing, the other children would say, 'We're not allowed to play with you Orange bastards.' It scared us because we were only young. I had seven sisters and one brother and the whole family felt the change happening. It just seemed to get worse and worse. Then Protestants all started to leave. I couldn't understand why everybody was leaving, but it wasn't long until we found out – they started putting lit matches through our front letterbox.

I remember many a night getting up to use the bathroom and seeing my father sitting there on the bottom stair, waiting. He wouldn't go to bed; he was so scared something would happen to us. In the end, he had to tell us the IRA had threatened us – and that Protestants had been warned to get out of Top of the Hill.

My father and mother loved living there and they were devastated. We had never had any problems with our neighbours, they were our friends – but this was a time when businesses were being bombed all over the town, and it just wasn't safe anymore. I remember my daddy crying about leaving. He was

Everything seemed to change overnight

so sad because we couldn't stay in our home, or maybe crying at the whole situation in general.

As a child, I couldn't understand it. We couldn't understand why they didn't want us to stay. The last straw was when they poured petrol through our letterbox and struck a match. It was caught just in time, and my daddy said we had to go. It was so sudden. We came in from school one day, and then we were gone. We didn't even get to say goodbye to anyone in the street, my daddy just told us that 'for our safety' we had to get out.

We had nowhere to go. Many Protestants were squatting in the new half-built houses in Clooney, so that's where we ended up, too. The house wasn't finished, but we had no choice but to move in anyway. There was no electric, no footpaths, there were rats running up the walls. I remember the day we moved. It was at night and I got no homework done because we had no electric, but when my teacher found out I didn't do my homework, I got a hammering – and it wasn't even my fault.

> I couldn't understand why everybody was leaving, but it wasn't long until we found out – they started putting lit matches through our front letterbox.

It felt as though we were thrown out of Top of the Hill – 'Protestants not allowed'. I know some Catholics feel that this was done to them, but it was done to us in the 1970s, too. We weren't allowed to live there, and I feared for my parents' safety.

My father brought us up to treat others as we'd like to be treated ourselves, but then all of a sudden we come home from school one day, all our stuff is packed up and we're away. Our friends and neighbours didn't do this to us – they were good people. It was the hardliners who were responsible, not the ordinary Catholics.

It was awful in Clooney. We had no streetlights or footpaths, just muck and rats. We had to get the rat-man in, and I remember him letting us see the nests of baby rats. More and more people squatted there – they had no choice. They were scared and had to find somewhere fast.

Life settled down a bit after we moved, but then trouble started in our new area, too, and there were riots. My daddy wouldn't let us out the door once it was dark because of the two sides fighting, but we could see everything from our bedroom window anyway. One night, the police were firing rubber bullets and the boy next door was hit by one while out painting his fence and it broke his arm. I remember he kept the rubber bullet.

My daddy brought us up to do right and respect people. He was strict, but it did us no harm. My parents were both in the army years ago, and my sister and I dreamed of joining the navy – or so we thought – until my daddy got the papers and burnt them. I was so angry, but my father said no daughter of his would be joining the navy. He said women were treated like dirt. He was very protective of us, so maybe that's why he did it, but it still broke my heart. I ended up going into some shop to work instead. I could have been a sailor – I could have ended up in the Bahamas or somewhere.

When I worked in the supermarket, I knew a man there who worked for the bakery. He and I chatted every day, and he used to worry that he would be targeted because he was also part-time UDR. One day I was going to work, and there he was lying outside – dead. The IRA had shot him. He was such a gentleman – a hardworking, good man with two young sons – and he was shot just because he was in the UDR. I kept thinking about that poor man, his poor wife and wains.

It's a terrible thing to say, but that was part of our growing up – it was something we lived through and we grew used to. I have had many friends shot and killed by the IRA over the years.

I moved away at nineteen when I got married. Once, I went back to visit the little house that we were all brought up in. When my own children eventually asked about my childhood, I took them up to see it, too. They asked why we had left it, and I told them the truth – there's no point lying to them. I told them about the Troubles, and how it was safer for us to leave.

I've brought my children up to respect everybody. Back then, you couldn't even date a Catholic. If you ever did, you certainly never told anybody about it. You had to sneak around, and told nobody but your best friend or you'd be called a turncoat. You definitely weren't allowed to bring them into the estate, and then you worried when they walked home, too. There were no phones in those days to text and ask if they got home safe – you just had to wait until you saw them again to know for sure. That's how we lived. It was probably the same for the Catholic side, too. I'm sure they had to hide it if they were going out with a Protestant. It doesn't matter nowadays. I know lots of people in mixed relationships and it's no longer frowned upon.

I have four children now. We were watching TV one day when they showed footage of the Troubles and my daughter saw a building in town bombed. 'What's a bomb, Mammy?' she asked. She didn't even know what a bomb was, or why one would be used. She was only thirteen at the time, and I had to explain it somehow. I didn't know the first thing about them myself, but she was genuinely interested so I told her what I could.

After that, we took her out on a drive around the city, over the Fountain and into the Bogside. We told her the whole story about what happened here, and how we were not allowed over there when we were young – just to educate her a bit. It felt strange telling her these things. I still remember the first time I walked into the Bogside myself. I thought I was going to get battered. It didn't happen, obviously, but the fear was still there.

I don't know what the future holds for Northern Ireland because the politicians just can't agree. They can't even talk but they end up fighting. The government are failing us. It's not working, and I think the wrong people are in charge. I could probably do a better job myself.

My father always told us to bring up our children with manners, teach them right from wrong and the importance of respect, and we have done that. Two of my children still can't get jobs, though, and the politicians are sitting up there, earning big money and doing nothing. Our young people need more opportunities.

I'm not sure if there even is peace nowadays. We still have dissidents and now we have a terror threat from other extremists, too, and we don't want it. Things aren't as bad as they once were, I suppose. Life here is better now, and at least it teaches us to bring our children up well so this can never happen again.

Donna Porter

Nobody had it easy, but that's just the way it was

An ordinary day at work spiralled into a nightmare for young mother-of-five Donna Porter when two RUC officers were gunned down mere yards from where she worked in Derry/Londonderry's city centre. The incident has never been far from her thoughts since. Now seventy years old, she reflects on what she saw that day, and how the experience triggered a lifelong, debilitating fear of blood and raw meat.

I was witness to a murder. I saw a policeman being killed in 1982, when I had a cleaning job at a banking and insurance firm in the Diamond – before the Richmond Centre was built.

I was cleaning the windows when I noticed a van driving past. I had seen it before, and had said to my colleague, 'Isn't that wee van gorgeous,' so that's probably why I noticed it when I saw it again. When it came up around again, it stopped in the middle of the Diamond, and the next thing – a man all dressed in black with a balaclava got out and just started shooting.

Two RUC police officers were shot, and I ran out to them. I knew that the policeman was dead when he hit the ground – because part of his head was lying on the pavement – but the policewoman beside him was still alive. She was probably only about twenty or twenty-one and badly wounded in the stomach. I went to get a towel and ran back out to her again, but, by then, someone I worked with had taken over and told me to go back inside. He put the towel around her to cover her injuries, but I had already seen everything by then …

I went back into my work, but someone came and told me to go home. I walked home down Carlisle Road, and ended up wandering into Sproule's the jewellers, for no real reason. I was in a bad way. They actually had to take me home from there. I think I coped when it was actually happening, but when everything hit me, it hit me badly.

I just happened to be on the scene first. There was nobody around, nobody coming up Shipquay Street, nobody – just me. I saw everything that happened. The girl was crying, 'Somebody, please help me,' and I just had to help. Anyone would …

The girl survived. I went to visit her in intensive care, and they let me in to see her – but she didn't really remember what happened. She recovered, thank God. I often wonder what happened to her since.

I was on my own for those first few hours until the wains came home from school. I didn't tell them anything, I just told my husband. I wouldn't have wanted my children to know, they were far too young.

Detectives contacted me later that afternoon. They told me they knew who it was, but they had no proof. I described the minivan and told them everything I could. The gunman was totally dressed in black, and I remember he was wearing a silver watch. All I could say was that it wasn't a rifle. I've seen quite a lot of guns, because I have an aunt in America and there are guns in her house, but I still wouldn't know what was what. It was long, with holes in the barrel, and you could see the light flashing when he fired. The police did tell me that the van almost knocked someone down when they were getting away from the Diamond.

I didn't take any time off work. I went straight back, but I never looked out the window anymore. In fact, I only stayed in the job another month or two before moving on. I don't know if I could have coped with staying there any longer. I didn't talk about what happened very much in the weeks and months afterwards.

> If something like that happened again, I know I couldn't do the same to help – my fear of blood is so bad.

People weren't offered counselling or anything in those days, they just got on with it.

For years, I haven't been able to touch a piece of meat to cook it, because of the blood. I still can't eat red meat to this day, either. My daughter always had to put the meat in the pot because I can't even look at it.

It's the same if I see anybody hurt and blood coming out – I'm away. I can't handle it at all, even when my grandchildren fall and cut themselves. Once, my granddaughter had a nosebleed, it bled all over her, and I couldn't cope with it, it was awful. I saw his face in hers, if that makes sense, and oh, dear, a panic attack wasn't the word for it. That day was a nightmare.

I don't talk about it much because it does upset me. My children know, but they also know I don't want to discuss it. At the time, I might have spoken about it if I had the opportunity … I suppose it still affects me, so I probably should speak to someone now. Look how many years have passed and I still can't talk about it or see blood.

In fact, if something like that happened again, I know I couldn't do the same to help – my fear of blood is so bad. I really love watching those CSI police programmes on TV, but I have my eyes closed every time there's blood on the screen.

I have memories of another incident, too. I was leaving my daughter to school one day when I saw a commotion at Frank Long's supermarket, and a breadman had been shot. We saw him taken out and into the ambulance. People were standing around watching, but I cleared out of there. I needed to get away.

We might be living in a peaceful society, but, honestly, I don't see that much has changed. There are people trying to get on with their lives, but there will always be bad elements around. I would like to see everyone get on, and no conflict at all, but I cannot see it happening in my lifetime. Nobody had it easy, but that's just the way it was.

There should be more opportunities to talk about things. There are days I can talk about what I saw and not cry at all, but then there are other days, too. I do still think about it, and I can't help but wonder what happened to the girl ...

Anonymous

Nothing has changed – people still live in fear

Within the confines of the North's 'peaceful' new society, there are still voices that go unheard amid the noise of politics. 'Eileen', who prefers to remain anonymous, is a woman born and bred in Derry's nationalist Creggan estate. Disillusioned by the peace process, Eileen is regarded by some as a 'dissident' republican – a title she refutes. Here, she speaks of her early years, the importance of community and remaining a proud republican in modern Derry.

There were thirteen of us reared in one house with my granny and granda. Those who I called my brothers and sisters were actually my aunties and uncles, but I still call them my brothers and sisters to this day.

My first memory of the conflict was the trouble starting in 1968, when I was about eleven years old. My grandparents were originally from the Lecky Road area and we still had relations there, and when the B-Specials went into The Wells and broke all the windows, people started to panic and many flocked to our house. We had no room, so we were like sardines in the beds.

When I turned fourteen, I was allowed into town to watch all the craic at the riots. That's how I met my husband – he was a rioter and we met during a riot in William Street. He was a brilliant stone-thrower, you see. We were going steady by the time I was fifteen and I was married at sixteen.

Back then, the rioting had spread to Creggan, too, and we used to meet at the riots – that was our date. When we were going steady and he was seventeen, I heard he'd been shot in the back at a riot. The army said he was a nail bomber. Thankfully, they had only hit him in the leg, but to this day, he still has operations on it. He wasn't even rioting that day, he was walking to the shop and they shot him from behind. After that, the Brits threw him in the back of the army jeep and drove around Creggan, with his legs hanging out of the jeep, so everyone could see he had been shot.

I was always being stopped and searched at checkpoints around the town. One time, I was heavily pregnant with my older girl, and the army ordered me to open my coat to be searched. I refused and was taken to Piggery Ridge base where they kept me for a couple of hours.

A woman eventually came in, and I agreed to open my coat for her, so they released me. But it was a matter of principle – I was opening my coat for no man.

Another time, the Brits lifted me because I gave them my name in Irish. My granda came up to get me out, saying, 'You have my granddaughter in there,' and they said, 'No, we have a foreigner.' He knew by that statement that I had given my name in Irish, and he wasn't a bit happy.

> There are houses and families still being raided in Creggan to this day – but it's never reported or talked about. Nobody wants to know.

I was always politically minded, probably more so than my husband. I remembered my granny telling me stories of her father – my great-grandfather – who was excommunicated from the Catholic Church for being a member of the IRA many years before. She would tell me stories about him and what they went through while we peeled the potatoes in the kitchen. I loved listening, and that's how I became interested in Irish history.

With life how it was, all my interests in politics fell by the wayside. I reared my children and worked in the factory. It was a hard struggle sometimes. We were brought up to believe you stayed married until the day you died, so I was shocked when my husband walked out on me. We were older by then, and our children were all grown-up, but it was still a shock. In hindsight, it was the best thing that ever happened to me.

Of course, I crumbled and fell apart for about a year or so, but I knew it was for the best. I wished I had the confidence to have done it myself years ago, but I worried I wouldn't be able to manage, because I'd been on medication for years – the same stuff they give prisoners to calm them down.

My daughters were a great support. We're really close and fairly open and honest about everything, good or bad. The birth of my grandson was the biggest turnaround in my life. I was in and out of Gransha Hospital with depression and suddenly I realised that I had something worth fighting for – something so positive to focus on. I was never in Gransha again.

Thinking back on my life, I wish I had been a lot stronger. I do feel much stronger these past few years, but I still have my weaknesses. Sometimes I have down days and I feel like I'm falling down, struggling. Sometimes I can see no future.

Nothing has changed – people still live in fear

I was delighted with the peace process when it happened, but it hasn't worked. Nothing has really changed for me or my friends or the communities we live in. We're actually worse off now, because nobody will speak out about things that continue to happen nowadays. Is it any wonder we've lost faith in the peace process?

There are houses and families still being raided in Creggan to this day – with children squealing and crying inside – but it's never reported or talked about. Nobody wants to know.

During raids, we stand outside houses supporting the families, letting them know we're there for them and that they're not alone. The very fact that someone is invading their home is excuse enough to go and show support, even if their own next-door neighbours won't come out. Wives and children are not to blame for this – they're raided because of whoever they're attached to or married to.

People still live in fear here, be it fear of cops or fear of benefit cuts. So many people in my area are on benefits and worried sick that they'll lose them. People say Creggan is full of people on disability allowance, but Creggan lived through a war and every single person on that estate was touched by it – so it's no wonder so many people are screwed up; no wonder so many are on tablets or benefits. If we lived in England, we would all be getting counselling today for trauma, but here nobody cares. We're just forgotten about.

People are still afraid to speak out because they'll be labelled a dissident. I'm not a dissident – I just stopped supporting Sinn Féin and I was honest about that. Now I've been labelled, even though I supported Sinn Féin all my life.

People are fed up. They've had enough of how things are. They are worried about bedroom tax and cuts to benefits; they are worried about housing and living in inadequate homes with mouldy walls. I care about the community, the people around me. Someone has to.

Anonymous

Burnt out of our home – by our friends

Escalating unrest during the latter part of the 20th century saw many families – both Catholic and Protestant – displaced from their respective communities. This growing divide proved disastrous for one family living peacefully in Top of the Hill, adjacent to a well-known sectarian flashpoint in Derry/Londonderry.

I was born a Protestant in Derry, and I grew up in Top of the Hill. My parents were very strict and hardworking: my mother fostered children and my father worked in a shop. Respect was a word that was always beat into us, but I was a happy child, skipping down Chapel Road every Sunday, going to Sunday school.

As we got older, you could see the divide starting between Protestants and Catholics. The British soldiers were suddenly everywhere on the streets. I was probably nine or ten then, and you could feel something happening. Protestant families were made to feel so unwelcome that they started moving out of Top of the Hill, but we were okay. We had great neighbours and we were happy enough where we were.

There was a bonfire on 15 August every year, and we lived right next door to the field where it was held. We often stood around the bonfire with everyone else, and it was always great fun. One year, when I was about twelve years old, things turned nasty. On this particular occasion, tensions were high and we were burnt out of our home – by our own friends and neighbours. We were the last Protestant family left in Top of the Hill …

They had actually started burning our fence, and my mother took fear, realising what was happening. People around the bonfire started calling us 'Orange bastards'. I just remember the hatred and aggression for Protestants that night.

I'll never forget my mother, who was going blind by then, putting me out the back bedroom window so I could run down for help to my father's work. He closed up the shop, and by the time we got up home, the crowd was hostile. My parents took what they could with them, whatever clothes we had on us and some other things. I never went back to the house. To me, we were an easy target.

Burnt out of our home – by our friends

The police shipped us out that night to emergency housing elsewhere. It broke my heart. I loved Top of the Hill, and I was leaving all my friends, my home, everything was upside down. It was terrible to be snatched away from my home like that.

They were our friends and neighbours. *My friends ...* To actually watch it happen, to see how your neighbours could turn against you because of your religion. That made me a very bitter person. My parents took it all very badly, too. My da hit the drink, and we all suffered for that. He would come in drunk and would take it out on us and we would get whaled.

> Suddenly, they were Catholics, I was a Protestant, and that was that.

We ended up in a children's home in County Tyrone before being moved to a home in Derry with the nuns. My mother ended up in Gransha Psychiatric Hospital and my father was on the drink, so we had nobody. The nuns were actually very good to us, but once, I ran away to where my daddy was working and told him I wasn't going back there. My father said, 'Well, I don't want you,' and the police came and took me back to the home. We were in the home for about six weeks until my mother got out of Gransha and brought us to her house.

I hated our new neighbourhood. It was just an environment I didn't want to be in. Moving to an all-Protestant area exposed me to a lot of bitterness against Catholics, and you heard the language they used, calling them 'Fenian bastards'. When you run around with a bunch of Protestants, you do what they do to fit in.

Even after we moved, I kept going back to Top of the Hill because it was all I knew. I'll never forget the day that I stopped going into my old area, though. My friend and I were walking to the shop one day to buy a single fag. On the way there, a man I knew very well grabbed me by the school tie and said, 'See you, you Orange bastard, *never* put your foot back in Top of the Hill!' I knew then that my days there were finished. I was gutted. There was no going back after that. Suddenly, they were Catholics, I was a Protestant, and that was that. I remember thinking if I had a gun I would have taken it to Top of the Hill, I was *that* angry. Thank God, I didn't have access to a gun. I was only a child anyway.

Nowadays I work in the community, particularly with women in my area, trying to make our community a better place. We know it hasn't all gone away since the Good Friday Agreement, but I can honestly see a big difference. Not in all areas, because some people can't let go, but that's up to them, isn't it?

This time two years ago, I would have been a much angrier person, although I was mellowing with age. I didn't even know where Creggan was, and I certainly would never have gone over there. I thought I would get my head kicked in. I know women who had never set foot outside the Waterside, certainly not in Creggan, and now some are going there, meeting new people and visiting places they'd never have imagined.

Sometimes you do wonder if you're making a difference, but I do see progress. And as I work more and more with different communities, I now see there are two sides to every story.

Siobhan Gallagher

Nobody is listening to our concerns

Irish families are renowned for their strength and resilience and this fortitude often passed down through the generations. Such is the case with three generations of one Derry family – Siobhan Gallagher (née Meenan), her daughter Amie Gallagher and their mother and grandmother, Sadie McGrory, now in her eighties. As part of the oral history strand of Unheard Voices, Siobhan and Amie Gallagher trace family influences and reflect on life in Derry today.

I come from a family of seven children. My father, Jackie, died when I was seven; he died of cancer the week before Christmas in 1968. What I remember most about it was crying because I wanted to go to school to get a bag of sweets that day.

I was always a mammy's girl, even when my father was alive, and I still am today. As teenagers, we would have had our moments, but my mother and I were still really close. She never had any favourites and treated us all equally. We got new clothes at Christmas and Easter, not like some parents today who seem to be out buying clothes every day of the week. We always sat at the kitchen table for our dinner, too; that was important. We weren't allowed to sit in the living room, and we always had a good staple diet.

We didn't have a lot of money. Although my mother was widowed, she always had to pay for our meals and wasn't entitled to anything. If she came home from town with a new piece of clothing, you wanted it. You appreciated things when you got them, and if you didn't want it, then someone else took it and was glad of it.

She would have been quite responsible and strict with us, but not too strict. I think that's where the women in our house get their strength from – she was a very moral and strong woman. Just over five-foot tall, but if she said no, she meant no. You didn't ask a second time.

My mother's name is Sadie, and she's eighty-two now. She was born in 1931, and they didn't think she would survive at the time, but she's still here and in great health. Her brothers and sisters all died long ago, but she's still going strong and sometimes we joke she has a better social life than us.

I didn't get married until my mid-twenties, and so when I was younger I spent a lot of time with my mother, just sitting watching TV, talking and asking her things. I definitely think my own mother influenced how I brought up my own daughter, Amie. I like to think that it's all the moral and positive influences we are passing down from one generation to the next. I remember someone telling me when I was younger, 'You're better than nobody, and nobody's better than you,' and that's something I have always said to my own children, too.

> I didn't think things like that happened anymore, the stop and searches and house searches, until it started happening to me ... It feels like a violation to have them going through my personal belongings.

The army were everywhere in those days. You still went about your life, and, unless there were riots or something, they didn't bother you and you didn't bother them. There were checkpoints everywhere – at every entrance to the town: Carlisle Road, Strand Road, William Street, Bishop Street, Butcher Gate; I think Abercorn Road had one, too. They would deliberately pick out someone and embarrass them, nearly stripping them down to search them. Babies' prams were often searched, too; they even searched in nappies and emptied out people's baby bags.

Even when you were leaving the town, you were searched on the way out – that's just the way things were. No matter who you were, you were searched. It was normal. We still went out at nights, and we just knew to run if we heard shooting, but we had no option but to get on with our lives.

We'd go to watch the riots from faraway, too, although it was only to see the talent and craic really. One time I got a bit too close, and we were stuck in the middle of the riot. They were scooping people, and a jeep came towards us and almost went over the top of me. I literally froze, my feet wouldn't move and I had to be yanked out of there. That was the closest I ever came to being caught in the middle of the trouble. I probably would have been dead if someone hadn't pulled me in. My mother only found out a few years ago that this even happened.

Some houses in our street were raided over and over again. They'd pull everything out of the house, furniture, mattresses, everything. In one house, I remember a six-year-old girl had to go to the toilet, and the Brit walked her into the toilet with a gun pointed at her. It was terrible. We were quite lucky in that I was eighteen or nineteen years old before we were raided ourselves, but we were only raided once or twice and that was it.

During the Troubles, we knew to stay out of particular areas of the city, too. My mother had the same fears I did about the Fountain, the Waterside and certain places outside Derry. Things did happen at times, and you didn't want to tempt fate. Even now, I wouldn't sleep if I thought any of my children were over in the Waterside. I know it's only a handful of those living there who might cause trouble, but it does still intimidate you.

Although we're supposed to have peace now, my family has faced a lot of police harassment over the past year, and that is upsetting. I didn't think things like that happened anymore, the stop and searches and the house searches, until it started happening to us. Our home has been labelled as dissident and has been raided three times in the past year, with family members arrested on a number of occasions. It feels like a violation to have them going through my personal belongings. Now, every time I hear the police are nearby, I wait on them to land at my door – and it has left me with anxiety.

I'm disappointed at the silence from some in the community who might have condemned such police tactics in the past – and I feel that nobody is listening to our concerns. As a mother, I'm upset that the next generation is experiencing similar things to my own.

Amie Gallagher

Finding a voice in 21st-century Ireland

Northern Ireland's younger generation still feels remnants of the sectarian divide despite the relative peace of recent years. Amie Gallagher grew up in one of the city's most economically deprived areas, but with the support of her close-knit family and a passion for change, she dedicated herself to making her community a better, fairer place. Today, the mother-of-three advises local schools and women's groups on human rights and women's rights, and she has even delivered a talk to the US Congress.

I grew up in Creggan in the 1990s, and, looking back, I suppose aspects of the Troubles were still all around us, but it was just normal to us. People's houses being raided also seemed normal. I was aware of some people's parents being in jail, and seeing things like 'Free the POWs' written on walls everywhere.

We always attended the Easter commemorations in the cemetery, and I loved seeing all the bands. The army were always around, too, and I remember we'd be fascinated with their guns, even though we were warned to stay away.

The Bloody Sunday parade passed through our street every year, so I was aware of that from a very young age. I never really understood it, but I remember being amazed at the numbers of people on the march and all the banners and bands. Everyone put out a black flag that day, too.

When I was younger, I knew absolutely nothing about the Protestant community. I realise now that there were lots of people in our family and neighbourhood who were Protestant, but growing up they seemed to be these 'other' people who lived across the water. Orange marches and riots stick out in my mind, and the fact that we had to avoid the town at certain times of year, too.

It wasn't until I went to secondary school that I became aware of where I lived and that Creggan wasn't exactly perceived as a 'normal' area. Some people made a difference with me because of where I was from. I started to notice that many other people my age weren't really aware of the conflict, or even of Bloody Sunday – that's when I began to realise the impact that growing up in Creggan had on me.

I went to a party in the Waterside once, and we were asked to leave the party because of who we were and where we were from. Then when we got a

Finding a voice in 21st-century Ireland

taxi, the driver wouldn't leave us back into the cityside, either – he left us at the end of the bridge. We couldn't believe it.

We weren't brought up political, we were just educated about what went on. My daddy always had the news on in our house and was always talking about current affairs. His brothers were all very into reading, too, particularly history and political books, so I think that definitely influenced me.

I grew up knowing that my daddy was in jail a long time ago, but I didn't really understand why. I knew other people's parents had been in jail, so it was nothing to question. At school, I became friends with a girl and found out her father had also been in jail. I remember other people not seeing this as normal, so it cemented our friendship from an early age.

It was around this time that I started to ask my father questions, and I began to understand what it was like for my parents' generation growing up. My daddy never really talks about being in jail. I found articles about what happened at the time and I gave them to him to read. He took them, but he made nothing of it. He's the quiet man; you only get bits of information here and there.

When I went to Queen's University to do a degree in International Studies, I finally got to know people from the Protestant community. For the first time, I heard about their lives and their fears. Living in the student area in Belfast was a bit like living in a bubble. I had friends in North Belfast, and hearing their life stories encouraged me to study the conflict here more. It also made me realise how close the communities in Derry are.

> Meeting and working with loyalist ex-prisoners, or members of the PSNI, for example, was a steep learning curve for me. I had to question my own beliefs and values.

When I had my children, I came back to live in Creggan. Being a parent, I appreciated my community even more, but I also noticed issues and inequalities that still existed because of our past. I was let go from my job while I was on maternity leave. I was a single parent and struggled with depression for a time, but my mammy and family really helped me get back to myself. I decided to use this time I had while I was unemployed to volunteer and find out what I really wanted to do.

I volunteered with Derry's Peace and Reconciliation Group and met people from all sides of the community. Meeting and working with loyalist ex-prisoners, or members of the PSNI, for example, was a steep learning curve for me. I had to question my own beliefs and values. I did, and still do, class myself as republican, but I realised that I stereotyped certain groups because I didn't know them and hadn't heard their story. The time I spent working there confirmed my passions in working to address the effects of the conflict. In November 2012, I began volunteering as a researcher with a human rights organisation called the Pat Finucane Centre. Being in this kind of environment and hearing so many victims' stories highlighted the hurt that existed.

I've also been lucky to participate in community courses and training through Creggan Neighbourhood Partnership, the Community Foundation for Northern Ireland and now Creggan Enterprises' Unheard Voices Programme. Through these, I have met a variety of people and have begun to understand a lot more. Now I'm certain that working at the community level, particularly in Creggan, is where my passion lies.

Recently I was afforded the opportunity to go to Washington, and being from a marginalised/excluded group, it was fantastic to be chosen to go and speak directly to the Irish embassy, State Department and Congress about what is really going on at the grass roots here.

In my own community, there is now more intra-community tension than anything else. My family are now labelled as dissident, my mother's home has been searched and some of my relatives have been arrested. It's difficult at times to remain positive about the type of work I'm now engaged in while all this is going on.

I still have reservations about working with the police, too, and I'm not sure if that will ever change. However, working with Unheard Voices and going to Washington has given me the chance to pursue what I want without having to hide my beliefs or reservations.

Widows of War

It's sad that it took so long for us to talk about it. We were never offered counsellors at the time. We felt like the only people in the world who had lost someone. Nobody wanted to listen to us or cared what we had to say. Our own community and neighbours were the only ones to help us.

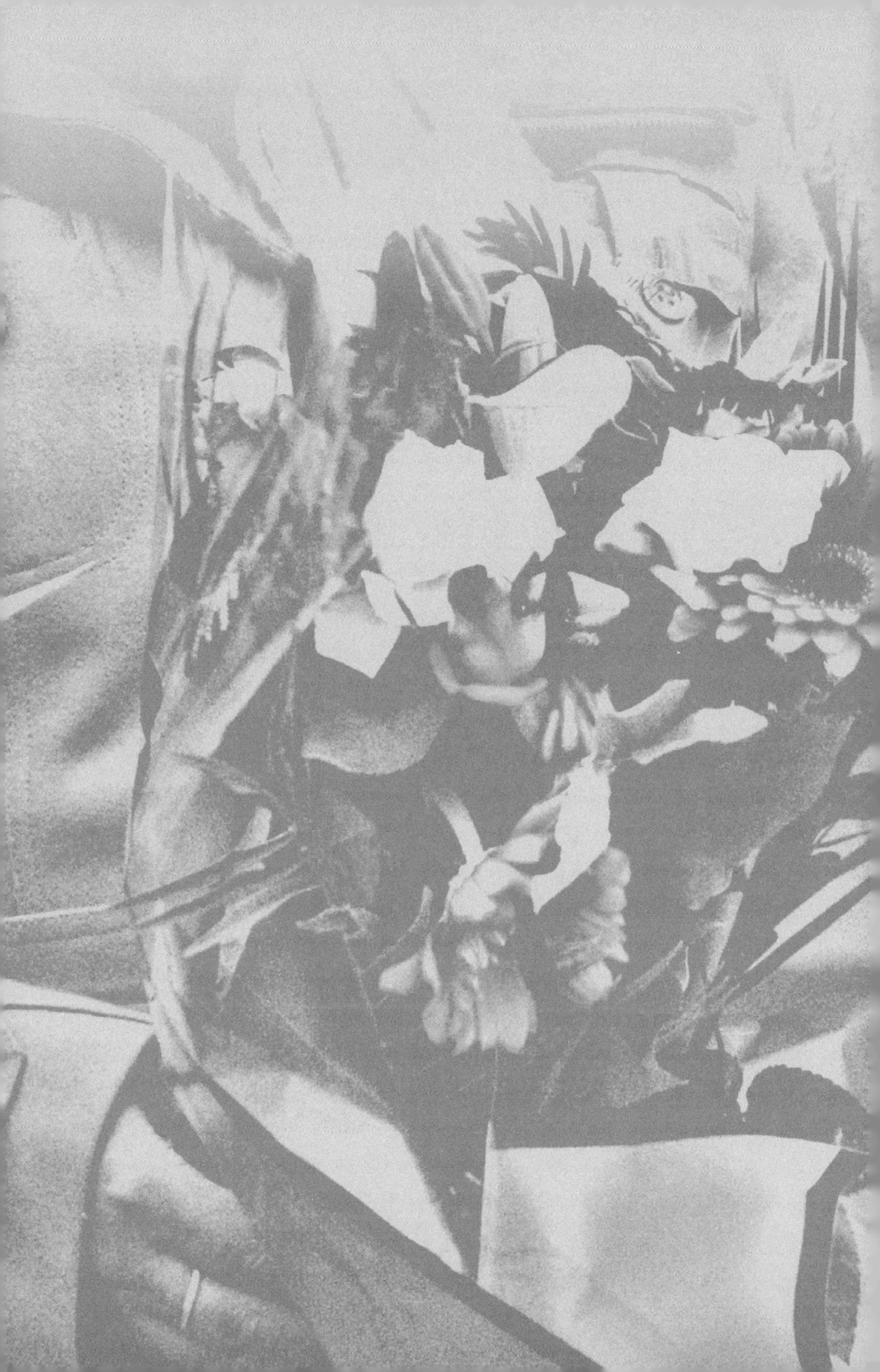

Anonymous

We don't talk about the past at all

Mother-of-two 'Sylvia' (not her real name) saw her husband murdered by paramilitaries in the family home. The experience decimated all their lives. Until now, Sylvia has never spoken to anyone, including her own children, about that night or its repercussions. All names have been changed in the following account.

Some weeks before my husband's murder, the police came to our house to let him know his name was on a paramilitary list that they'd found.

Then, one evening we were all at home and the children were upstairs. It was a wet night, and we brought our dog inside for shelter. 'Keith' and I were in the living room when a masked gunman appeared outside and shot Keith through the window. He didn't know what hit him and was knocked to the ground with the force of the bullet.

I sat there – frozen – staring at this man outside pointing a gun right at me. I couldn't move. I don't know what I thought; I just stared for a moment. I doubt I even screamed. He pointed that gun straight at me. I'm not sure if I was a target, too, but he fired more than once and there were bullets in the wall right behind me. I thought for a second maybe Keith had heard the shots and dived away, but one of the bullets had gone right through the armchair and ripped through his stomach. He was dead.

We had no phone in the house and I had to knock next door, but nobody answered. They were too scared. It seemed an eternity before someone eventually answered and got us an ambulance.

The children were upstairs, but they ran down when they heard the noise and saw their father lying there. I was quite calm, more shocked than in hysterics, because I rang my sister and said, 'Would you come and lift the children, Keith's been shot.' Even when I came home from the hospital that night, I still didn't cry. It was as if it had happened to someone else.

The children must have come in and sat with their father while I went out to look for help or a phone. They were both under ten – too young to see something like that.

At the hospital, nobody said it aloud but I knew Keith was dead. It was an hour or more before someone confirmed what I already knew. That night, after I came back from the hospital, the forensics team were still searching the

We don't talk about the past at all

house. When they had finished, friends of mine went in and tried to clean up the blood and mess before they'd let me go back in. I remember there were circles drawn in marker around all the bullet holes on the walls.

I stayed in the house that night and during the funeral. Once the funeral was over, I was out of there. I closed the door that night, and knew I was never going back. I didn't want to live in that house ever again. When we moved out of the house, we needed our furniture and so we had to take the sofa with the bullet hole with us. My children wanted to know why there was a hole in the sofa …

I went back to work two weeks later because we needed the money. If I hadn't had my parents, my sister Kelly and one or two friends, I would have been lost. They were the only support I had. My boss was more than good to me, too, so I just worked hard and tried to make a new life for us.

I was so bitter after Keith died that my children knew not to talk about it. We never discussed it. They didn't want to go out and play because they didn't want to leave me, but I'd send them on out and tell them not to worry. I just wanted to protect them and get on with my life. When Keith was shot I just retreated into my own wee world. I used to wish someone would come and take care of us and pay all the bills.

> I can't shake the stigma of my old name and my old life, and I want to. At the time, police suggested we should move to England – but how could I? Everyone I love lives here.

It made me an alcoholic. My nerves were terrible, and I began having a drink to help me sleep and that escalated. I was never one for taking a drink, except maybe on Christmas Day, but nothing compared to the amount I would drink now. It was just an easy way to deal with things at the time. After Keith died, I threw myself into going out and socialising again, because I could. That didn't help with the drink.

It's a daily struggle to control the alcoholism. If I get upset, the slightest wee thing can trigger me off and I can drink and drink and go missing for days. I can never hold down a job, either, because drink gets the better of me in the end and I get sacked. I can be nasty with drink in me, too.

Sometimes I've been so full, I didn't know where I was. I could have ended up anywhere. That could be quite dangerous. Sometimes I won't answer my phone for days, but my sister knows not to worry too much now. She knows I'll be in touch when I get it out of my system.

I also have a terrible fear. If I see a parked van with men near it, I will go out of my way to avoid it. I think to myself, 'Are they waiting for me?' When I'm in a car, I also worry about who's behind me and whether they could shoot me.

My curtains are always closed, too, day and night, because my husband was shot through an open window. My son pulls them in the morning now, but soon he'll get married and I'll be at home on my own, and that worries me because he's here every night with me. I'm not brave. I don't answer my door at night time. It's been decades since it happened, but unless I knew someone was calling around, there's no chance I'd open my front door at night.

I don't tell anyone my name, either, in case someone recognises it from the newspapers. I can't shake the stigma of my old name and my old life, and I want to. At the time, police suggested we should move to England – but how could I? Everyone I love lives here.

I am so proud of the men my sons have become. Considering all they have been through, they have grown up to be great fellas and I know they could have turned out so much worse.

Someone told me recently that my son said on Facebook that he was hiding under his bed when his father was shot … I never knew that … God knows what they went through. I was a mess, so who could they talk to?

My boys and I never got counselling and we still don't talk about the past at all. Now that I have talked about it here, I won't mention it again, or read it back. I might let my children read this story someday. To help them understand more about me, and about what happened that night.

Marie Newton

We were only beginning our lives

Marie Newton (Toland) was thirty-five when her first husband and father to their seven young children, John Toland, was gunned down in his own pub in County Derry in November 1976. The UDA/UFF later claimed responsibility for John's murder and tried to claim he was an informant for the IRA. Now a grandmother and great-grandmother in her seventies, Marie contemplates the loss of her first love and the effect his murder had on their family.

John ran a pub in Eglinton called the Happy Landing. He had been a barman and so, of course, we jumped at the chance of running our own pub, and John was determined to make a success of it. I'd been married at nineteen, and we had seven youngsters together. The eldest was fourteen and my youngest daughter was seven.

John ran the bar all day, and his mother came and watched the youngsters in the evenings so I could go down to help him. We'd been there three years and had just built a new lounge in the pub. We had a very busy, very happy life – the best life in the world.

We lived near St Eugene's Cathedral on the edge of the Bogside, and that night, I had a rash on my face and rang John from home to say I'd not be in. He told me not to worry; he would call in one of the girls to work instead.

At 6.00pm, I got the phone call to say John was shot dead. It was a priest who rang me. 'Are you Mrs Toland?' he asked, 'John's been shot – he's dead.' I thought someone was having me on. Our Danny was upstairs doing his homework at the time, and he flew past me in the hall in his bare feet and ran out the door to the cathedral, beating on the parochial house door until Bishop Daly came out. Danny told him his father had been shot, 'My mother needs a priest,' so Bishop Daly ran over.

When I talk about it now, I go right back to that very night and live every minute over again. Fr Neil Carlin came, too, and he went away to phone to find out if it was true. He confirmed that John was dead. They'd shot the face off him. They had walked up to the bar counter and asked him, 'Are you John Toland?' 'I sure am,' my John said, and they just riddled him with bullets.

They shot him in the neck and blew the roof out of his mouth, they shot him in the stomach, which got his kidneys, the lot, and then a third time in his chest, too. He was destroyed, shot to bits. He was only thirty-six. If I had been there that night, God knows what would have happened. Both of us could have been shot, and then who would have looked after our wains?

The lights went out in the village after they shot John – and so the car was able to speed out and away and nobody saw anything or knew anything. Eleven people were drinking in the bar that night, yet nobody saw a thing. Did nobody notice these unmasked men coming in with guns? It was as if John was a nobody, that's how I felt.

Straight away, the UFF claimed the shooting through a local newspaper. They said it was because he was an informant for the IRA, that 'he gathered information from intoxicated Protestants and passed it on to the IRA.' It beggars belief.

I could have given them his nightly pattern – John left our house at 10.00am and he came in again at 11.30pm every night and always had his dinner at that time of night. He hadn't even a political thought. He was too busy for anything like that. He was trying to make enough money to retire when he was forty, and he would have, too. We were just a normal, innocent, hardworking family. We were only beginning our lives. If they'd only phoned and threatened him, that would have been enough – we would have given up everything and left. They didn't need to kill him.

For a month afterwards, I got these phone calls in the middle of the night. Of course, I'd answer the phone so late at night, thinking it could be something urgent. A man's voice would say, 'Is that you, Mrs Toland? You're a widow a week today – how does it feel?'

Then the next time, it was, 'You're a widow two weeks now – how does it feel?' Then the next week, and the next, too. I phoned the police and they put a tracer on my phone, but never found him. I can still hear that voice today, though. And I've kept my phone ex-directory to this day. There are some evil people out there.

Three or four weeks after John died, I went to the police and told them I desperately needed help. I poured my heart out to an officer I knew, and told him who I thought – who I knew – had set John up. I took that chance; I put myself at risk to do what felt right, but that was the last I ever heard of it.

Our house died. It was always filled with craic, life and laughter, but it became empty. We were like shells of people. Danny became the man of the house, and all the children took on a role and became responsible. They had to grow up fast. I lined all the children up after John was buried, and warned them, 'If one of you ever join an organisation and get into bother, it'll be

We were only beginning our lives

the death of me.' None of them did, thankfully. I'm sure they struggled, but nobody took it further. They listened to me.

John's mammy went to pieces, and she died soon after. His death had a ripple effect, and that ripple doesn't stop. His brother went into the River Foyle a few years later. I thought about killing myself, too, in the weeks after John died. Then I thought about my wains, and who would take care of them, and I got hold of my senses. That was the biggest hurdle I had to get over in my life. I can talk about things and reminisce now, but I was a useless wreck back then. Everything was a hurdle that I had to get over.

I remember after John died, my children became unkempt. I didn't even iron their clothes anymore. Until one day, my sister told me off, and said that John would turn in his grave if he saw how I was sending the wains out – that I was acting like a lazy loafer. I wanted to reach for her, but from that day on, my children went out with their shoes polished and their clothes smoothed.

Another of the big hurdles I had to get over was going to the cemetery all the time. I would go up there several times a day, sometimes in my nightclothes, and I had to get control of that. It still went on for about two months, though, until I just visited him once a day.

> If they'd only phoned and threatened him, that would have been enough – we would have given up everything and left. They didn't need to kill him.

My mammy and daddy had lived next door to us, and the only thing that had got me through all those terrible months after John died was my daddy coming to check in on me every night. My mother had just died the year before, and five months after John was shot, my father took a brain haemorrhage and died, too. He was only fifty-nine and I think it was the shock and pressure of everything that had happened. My daddy had to go and identify John after he died, and then seeing me the way I was after it all – he had a lot to cope with.

So just five months later, I had nobody. That was it. For a while, we all just sat around like hermits. Our four boys adored their granda and they took it bad. They felt like they were abandoned for a second time in losing him, too. I will never be able to repay Bishop Daly and Fr Carlin; they always made time to call in to see us. They came faithfully for months. Many a night Bishop Daly would call and say his prayers with the wains.

John and I weren't millionaires by any means, but we had actually made some money in the pub and we were comfortable. Then, within weeks, we were on benefits. Complete poverty. That was very hard, but it teaches you a lot about life. You can take anything on the chin after that – and that's what's important.

My second husband has been a lifeline to me. He has changed everything and I want for nothing. I'm so lucky I met Thomas and found happiness. We married in 1979 and my own children welcomed it because they were just so happy to see me moving on.

Thomas' sister was married to John's brother, so we knew each other and he knew John, but it was still a huge hurdle for me to think about a relationship. I was still only a young woman, but it was a strange situation to be in. When I lined up my children and told them I wanted to get married again, they were thrilled. One son said it was the happiest day of his life, knowing I was happy, because up until then he had heard me wailing and crying at night. I never knew that.

When Thomas and I had the baby, it was a godsend to my wains – they doted on him. It brought this house back to life. Thomas has always been a father figure without trying, and my girls have always called him Daddy. Now I have eight children, twenty-three grandchildren and seventeen great-grandchildren.

A few years ago, the Historical Enquiries Team (HET) contacted us about our case. They were good people; they listened to us and cared. They told us that there was definite collusion in John's killing. The HET report cleared John's name and said that he was 'ruthlessly murdered'. It concluded that the reason behind his murder, besides him being Catholic, was that the UDA wanted the bar for themselves – so he was murdered for religion and money.

The Pat Finucane Centre supported us through the HET process and it's only through all this that my children are finding out details. To me, the Pat Finucane Centre offered us a chance to talk about it. They offered to listen. Because of them and the HET, we all sat down together and actually talked about things. It was the first time we'd ever done that as a family.

It's sad that it took so long for us to talk about it. We were never offered counsellors at the time. We felt like the only people in the world who had lost someone. When John died, nobody wanted to listen to us or cared what we had to say. Our own community and neighbours were the only ones to help us.

I hadn't been back in Eglinton for nearly thirty-eight years, until last year. My sister had to collect her daughter from a pub and it turned out to be the Happy Landing. My sister panicked, so both of us got up the nerve to go. I felt I was ready to see it again. Besides, I didn't want to send my sister there on her own. I texted my son on the way there, 'I'm on my way to Eglinton village,' and he texted back saying, 'Please, Mum, don't do it …'

The pub is still called the Happy Landing, but you wouldn't recognise it nowadays. My niece then asked us to leave her two friends up the hills behind Eglinton, and my heart sank because that's the route the car took that night. Still, we took the girls up home, and I haven't looked back since. It felt like some kind of release to me to do all that. I was ready to get over that hurdle, and I think my sister knew that, too. I never shed a tear that night or since, and I felt relaxed the whole time. I was stronger than I thought. That was a real turning point for me, and my family have even noticed the change.

My children have never been back to the pub, but they are thinking about going there together at some stage, just once. Maybe they could go into the Happy Landing. They could have a drink to mark their daddy's birthday, and you never know, I might go with them.

Because of everything we've been through, I think I'm a very strong, hardy woman, and I have instilled that in my own children, too. I can see John's strength in all of them – they've inherited that. I know I would never have survived without them.

Glossary

B-Specials
A section of the Ulster Special Constabulary, a 100% Protestant auxiliary police force set up in 1920 and disbanded in 1970.

Battle of the Bogside
In the afternoon of 12 August 1969, a parade by the Apprentice Boys of Derry led to a riot as the marchers passed the Bogside. The RUC entered the Bogside in large numbers to quell the rioting with water cannons. In response, the rioters formed barricades and attacked the police with petrol bombs and stones, forcing them back. The riot lasted for three days and only ended when the British Army was brought in to replace the RUC on 14 August.

Bloody Sunday
Refers to the shooting dead by the British Army of thirteen civilians (and the wounding of another fourteen, one of whom later died) during a civil rights march in Derry on 30 January 1972.

Civil rights marches
From 1967 to 1972, Northern Ireland Civil Rights Association (NICRA) engaged in a programme of street demonstrations and civil disobedience, demanding the right to vote, an end to gerrymandering and allocation of housing on the basis of need. Demands were also made to repeal the Special Powers Act, disband the B-Specials, end discrimination in employment and, later, to end internment. NICRA's use of street protests as a tactic virtually ended after the NICRA-organised anti-internment march on 30 January 1972, which became known as Bloody Sunday.

Civil rights march – Duke Street, 5 October 1968
A civil rights march planned for 5 October was banned because of fears that it might clash with an Apprentice Boys' parade, but it went ahead, attended by 200-400 people. The march was stopped by the RUC in Duke Street in the Waterside, and a number of people were injured in the

ensuing trouble, including several MPs. The march and subsequent trouble received worldwide media coverage, putting Northern Ireland firmly in the headlines.

Collusion
Collusion is an umbrella term used to describe parties working together in an underhand or deceitful way by secret agreement. In the context of the Troubles, it encompasses the numerous cases of alleged – and proven – collusion between state agencies and paramilitary organisations in carrying out criminal activities in Northern Ireland. In one recent inquiry, collusion was defined as ranging 'from the wilful failure to keep records, the absence of accountability, the withholding of intelligence and evidence, through to the extreme of agents being involved in murder'. Three investigations into a number of murders here found evidence of collusion between state agencies in Northern Ireland and paramilitary groups. These agencies included the RUC, British military, and MI5.

Dissident
A term used to describe Irish republicans who are opposed to the Good Friday Agreement.

Fort George
Fort George was a large fortified Ministry of Defence (MOD) army base built on a former shipbuilding and repair site off the Strand Road. The waste ground became known as Fort George in 1969 when the army took control and it remained in MOD use until 2001 when it was transferred to the Londonderry Port and Harbour Commissioners.

Good Friday Agreement
The Belfast Agreement was a pivotal part of the Northern Ireland peace process, widely known as the Good Friday Agreement because it was reached on Good Friday, 10 April 1998. The agreement, between the Irish and British Governments and the majority of Northern Ireland's political parties provided a consensus for how the region should be governed. The agreement's aim was to establish a nationalist and unionist power-sharing government in Northern Ireland, and the talks leading up to it dealt with many issues that had caused conflict during the previous thirty years.

Greysteel Massacre
On 30 October 1993, six Catholics and a Protestant were killed and thirteen others injured in a UFF gun attack in the Rising Sun Bar at Greysteel, County Derry. The UFF claimed the Hallowe'en night attack was in response to the PIRA Shankill Bombing in Belfast which had taken place a week earlier with multiple deaths and casualties.

Guard of Honour
In the context of this collection, a guard of honour is a term describing the ceremonial act carried out during the funerals of Irish Republican Army (IRA) volunteers.

Historical Enquiries Team (HET)
In September 2005, the Police Service of Northern Ireland (PSNI) set up the Historical Enquiries Team to investigate the 3,269 unsolved murders committed during the Troubles. The new unit had three objectives: to work with families of those who had been killed, to ensure cases were investigated to modern policing standards and to gain public confidence.

Internment (Operation Demetrius)
Internment (imprisonment without trial) was introduced in August 1971 by the then Prime Minister of Northern Ireland, Brian Faulkner. In a series of dawn raids, the army attempted to arrest over 400 men they believed were connected to the IRA. However, very few of those arrested had any association with the republican movement at the time. This policy of internment led to a major upsurge in violence.

Loyalist
Refers to someone who is loyal to the British Crown. The term in a Northern Ireland context is used by many commentators to imply that the person gives tacit or actual support to the use of force by paramilitary groups to defend the union with Britain.

Nationalist
A term used to describe those who hold a long-term wish for the reunification of Ireland. The majority of those people who are from the Catholic community are nationalist. It should be noted that not all nationalists support republican groups.

Pat Finucane Centre (PFC)
Pat Finucane Centre is a human rights advocacy and lobbying group based in Northern Ireland, with offices in both Derry and Newry. The group, commonly known as the PFC, is named in honour of murdered Belfast solicitor Pat Finucane and promotes a nonviolent resolution of the conflict on the island of Ireland.

Piggery Ridge
Following Operation Motorman in July 1972 in Derry, the British Army established a number of bases in the Creggan area on the city's west bank, one of which was 'Piggery Ridge' near Creggan Heights – a frequent scene of confrontation. ('Motorman' was the name given to a massive military operation by the British Army to reclaim 'no-go areas' set up in towns across Northern Ireland.)

(P)IRA – Provisional Irish Republican Army
The dominant force in the Troubles. It originated in December 1969 when a split occurred due to the 'old' IRA Army Council voting in favour of giving recognition to the parliaments of Dublin, London and Northern Ireland. This was against traditional policy and the more militant elements opposed to this broke away and formed PIRA, normally referred to as the IRA.

PSNI – Police Service of Northern Ireland
Established in November 2001, the Police Service of Northern Ireland replaced the Royal Ulster Constabulary (RUC).

RAF – Royal Air Force
The Royal Air Force is Britain's military air force, founded towards the end of World War I in 1918 and more commonly known today as the RAF.

Republican
A general term used for those who wish to reunite Ireland and are prepared to use military methods. Mainly Catholic.

RUC – Royal Ulster Constabulary
The RUC were the unionist police force in Northern Ireland, set up after the partition in 1922 and renamed the Police Service of Northern Ireland in 2001.

Sinn Féin
A historic political movement which takes its name from the Irish meaning 'we ourselves', and which established itself as the political branch of the IRA. Founded in 1905, Sinn Féin sought to promote political and economic independence from England and, after partition, the unification of the island of Ireland. Today, Sinn Féin is the second largest party in the power-sharing Northern Ireland Executive, behind the Democratic Unionist Party.

Tear gas
For many decades, tear gas (or CS gas) has been used by police forces globally as a means of controlling civilian crowds. Though intended to deal with sieges, armed robberies or terrorist attacks, tear gas was frequently used against demonstrators at the height of the Troubles in Northern Ireland in the 1970s. Inhaling the gas caused a variety of temporary, unpleasant physical effects such as gagging and impaired vision.

Territorial Army (TA)
The Territorial Army (TA) is the active-duty volunteer reserve force supporting the British Army. Created in 1908, it was renamed the Army Reserve in 2013.

Tricolour
The tricolour is the national flag of Ireland, consisting of green, white and orange vertical stripes.

Twelfth Celebrations
General term used to describe the annual parades held by the Orange Order in Northern Ireland to celebrate prominent events in Protestant history. Nineteen main parades are held across Northern Ireland (with one in County Donegal) on or around 12 July every year, and in Derry/Londonderry the Apprentice Boys commemorate the Relief of Derry on 12 August, when the city was relieved after the Great Siege of 1688–89.

UDA – Ulster Defence Association
The largest Protestant paramilitary group, it was launched in 1971 as an umbrella body for loyalist vigilante groups which had sprung up around Belfast and surrounding areas amidst the growing violence at that time. In many loyalist districts, the UDA was seen as a replacement for the B-Specials and was organised very much along military lines.

UFF – Ulster Freedom Fighters
A cover name used by individuals linked to the UDA to claim certain paramilitary actions.

Unionist
A term used to describe those who wish to see the union with Britain maintained. The majority of those people who are from the Protestant community are unionist. It should be noted that not all unionists support loyalist groups.

Other useful information on the events, individuals and organisations involved in the Troubles is available at the Ulster University Conflict Archive on the Internet (CAIN) website: http://cain.ulst.ac.uk/